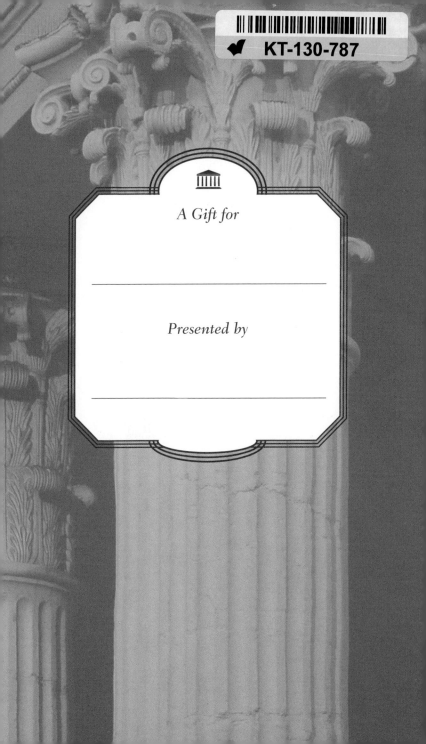

A Gift for

_____

Presented by

_____

The
Classics

"Education is learning what you didn't even know you didn't know."
—Daniel Boorstin, American historian

The Classics

All You Need to Know,
from Zeus's Throne
to the Fall of Rome

CAROLINE TAGGART

The Reader's Digest Association
New York/Montreal

A READER'S DIGEST BOOK

Copyright © 2010 Michael O'Mara Books Limited

First published in Great Britain in 2010 by Michael O'Mara Books
Limited, 9 Lion Yard, Tremadoc Road, London SW4 7NQ

READER'S DIGEST TRADE PUBLISHING
Consulting Editor: Barbara Webb
Manager, English Book Editorial, Reader's Digest Canada: Pamela Johnson
Project Production Coordinator: Wayne Morrison
Senior Art Director: George McKeon
Executive Editor, Trade Publishing: Dolores York
Manufacturing Manager: Elizabeth Dinda
Associate Publisher, Trade Publishing: Rosanne McManus
President and Publisher, Trade Publishing: Harold Clarke

Library of Congress Cataloging in Publication Data

Taggart, Caroline, 1954–
    The classics : all you need to know, from Zeus's throne to the fall of Rome /
Caroline Taggart.
        p. cm.
    Includes bibliographical references.
    ISBN 978-1-60652-132-8
    1. Civilization, Classical. 2. Civilization, Greco-Roman. 3. Classical languages. 4.
Classical literature. 5. Mythology, Classical. 6. Science, Ancient. 7. Philosophy,
Ancient. 8. Games—Greece. 9. Games—Rome. I. Title.
    DE59.T34 2010
    938—dc22

                                    2009049746

Reader's Digest is committed to both the quality of our products and the service we provide
to our customers. We value your comments, so please feel free to contact us: The Reader's
Digest Association, Inc., Adult Trade Publishing, 44 S. Broadway, White Plains, NY 10601

For more Reader's Digest products and information, visit our website:
www.rd.com (in the United States)
www.readersdigest.ca (in Canada)

Printed in the United States of America

3 5 7 9 10 8 6 4 2

Acknowledgments

My heartfelt thanks, again, to Silvia, Ana, Toby and everyone else at Michael
O'Mara for making these books happen; to Jamie Buchan and Dan Crompton
for enthusiastic nit-picking; to Glen for designing at the speed of light; and to
the enormous number of friends and relations who seem to have got almost as
much enjoyment out of the whole experience as I have. A friend when you're
having fun is a friend indeed.

Contents

Before I Begin...

Two things: a decision and a question.

The decision, with a book like this, is what to include and what to leave out. For most people, "classical" means the Ancient Greeks and Romans, and I have stuck to them except when they came up against people such as the Persians or the Carthaginians who couldn't be ignored. The first great Greek writer was Homer, in around the ninth century B.C., while the last great Roman ones wrote in the second century A.D.; most of the famous philosophers, inventors, politicians and emperors lived in between. Obviously the mythology came before Homer—because that is what he was writing about—and the Roman Empire went on for a bit longer, so don't hold me to those dates, but they are my rough parameters.

The question is, "Who cares?" After all, it was all a very long time ago, it has no relevance to us, and it isn't as if the Greeks and the Romans were the world's first civilizations anyway. And it's all sooo boring... isn't it?

True, Buddha and Confucius both died before Socrates was born, so the Greeks can't claim to have invented philosophy. As anyone who saw the Tutankhamen exhibition knows, the Egyptians were doing some pretty sophisticated stuff with gold in the fourteenth century B.C., and building pyramids over a thousand years before that. The Babylonians created huge stepped structures known as ziggurats, and topped them off with temples, in around 2000 B.C.; the Assyrians had magnificent palaces by 800 B.C. The Sumerians had a written language as early as 3500 B.C., as did the Hittites 2,000 years later—but that was still 600 years or more before anything was written down in Greek. So the Greeks didn't invent art, architecture or culture, either. Why all the fuss?

I suppose the answer is that they invented *our* art, architecture, culture and philosophy. In the twenty-first-century Western world, there are classical influences all around us. A civic building that looks serious and important is likely to be in the classical style. Whether we know it or not, we put together a logical argument following principles laid down by Aristotle. We do geometry and trigonometry because the Ancient Greeks showed us how. (Perhaps not the strongest argument in their favor.) Our language is full of references to *Herculean tasks* and having *the Midas touch*. Judges still *ad lib*, comedians hold sessions *in camera*—or should that be *vice versa*? Even if we don't study the classics, there's simply no getting away from them.

Unlike most of the earlier Middle Eastern civilizations, the Greeks and Romans also left us a massive amount of writing. We know what their lives were like, we know about their wars and their politics, their crimes and misdemeanors, their wives and lovers. Quite a lot more than is any of our business about their lovers, actually. We know that they were just like us. Lines such as "We are just statistics, born to consume resources" might have been written yesterday, and "You may drive out nature with a pitchfork, yet she'll be constantly running back" might have come straight from the mouth of British broadcaster and gardener Alan Titchmarsh. Yet they are both Horace, writing (and gardening, evidently) in the first century B.C.

Which brings me to the not insignificant point that the classical writers are fun. Admittedly there aren't many laughs in the Greek tragedies, but anyone who tells you that the classics are dull hasn't read Herodotus, Ovid, Horace or Tacitus, or seen the plays of Euripides or Sophocles performed. And, if I may mention this without lowering the tone too much, Aristophanes, Catullus and Juvenal all produced a considerable amount of pure filth that still has the power to amuse or arouse.

Until very recently, the classical world was an integral part of our education system. Less than a century ago, George Bernard Shaw could call a play *Pygmalion* and expect his audience to understand why. Yet over the past twenty years, the number of students taking Latin has diminished and almost nobody learns Greek. It seems a shame, because there is so much in the classics that speaks to us today.

Still, *nil desperandum*. Perhaps some of the snippets in this book will encourage you to seek *bona fide* sources and overturn the *status quo*. As for me, this introduction was the last bit of the book to be written, so *nunc est bibendum*—in other words, I've finished, so I'm off to have a glass of wine.

1

The Wordy Stuff: Classical Languages

At a conservative estimate, about half of modern English derives from Latin, and a lot of that has Greek origins, with the result that just under a third of the words in an average English-speaker's vocabulary are ultimately drawn from Greek. So, though few people learn either language these days, and most of us would be hard pressed to tell an ablative from an aorist, we nevertheless babble away in these ancient tongues all the time.

But it has to be said that there is something slightly off-putting about your first glance at Greek…

The Greek alphabet

This is a very different beast from the Roman alphabet we use today, although the Romans developed theirs from a classical Greek original.

Greek letter	Symbol	English equivalent
Alpha	A, α	a
Beta	B, β	b
Gamma	Γ, γ	g
Delta	Δ, δ	d
Epsilon	E, ε	e (as in *met*)
Zeta	Z, ζ	z or ds (as in *gods*)
Eta	H, η	e (as in *meet*, sometimes as in *may*)
Theta	Θ, θ	th
Iota	I, ι	i
Kappa	K, κ	k
Lambda	Λ, λ	l
Mu	M, μ	m
Nu	N, ν	n
Xi	Ξ, ξ	x
Omicron	O, o	o (as in *hot*)
Pi	Π, π	p
Rho	P, ρ	r
Sigma	Σ, σ	s
Tau	T, τ	t
Upsilon	Y, υ	u
Phi	Φ, φ	ph
Chi	X, χ	ch (as in *loch*)
Psi	Ψ, ψ	ps
Omega	Ω, ω	o (as in *slow*)

Most people are content to sail through life without worrying about this, but if you do any amount of math or science, you will come across π, ρ, θ and many others; if you read the Bible, you will find "I am Alpha and Omega, the beginning and the ending"—which is just the Greek way of saying "I am A and Z, not to be confused with a street directory"; and if you are an outstanding scholar in the United States, you might be honored with the **ΦΒΚ** (Phi Beta Kappa) award. That said, what really matters to most of us are not the letters but the words.

A touch of logorrhea

That's a fancy word for "verbal diarrhea," and just to prove the point that it is not all Greek to any of us, here are some examples of everyday words with Greek roots.

Asterisk	*asteriskos* (little star)
Biology	*bios* (life) *logia* (study)*
Catastrophe	*kata* (down) *strophe* (turning)
Clone	*klon* (twig, i.e., from which a new plant is created)
Democracy	*demos* (people) *kratos* (rule)
Dyslexia	*dys* (impaired) *lexis* (word)
Economy	*oikos* (house) *nemein* (to manage)
Geography	*ge* (earth) *graphein* (to write)
Helicopter	*helikos* (spiral) *pteron* (wing)
Hippopotamus	*hippos* (horse) *potamos* (river)
Homeopathy	*homoios* (similar) *pathos* (suffering)
Horoscope	*ora* (time) *skopein* (to observe)
Monogamy	*monos* (one) *gamos* (union)
Pantomime	*pantos* (all) *mimos* (mimic)†
Rhinoceros	*rhinos* (nose) *ceros* (horn)
Telephone	*tele* (far) *phone* (voice)
Xenophobia	*xenos* (stranger) *phobos* (fear)
Zoo	*zoion* (animal)

---

* And all sorts of other *bio-* words such as *biography, biosphere, biodegradable,* and *-ologies* such as *geology, astrology, sociology, theology.* See? You learn one thing and you find you know lots more.

† There are lots of other *pan-* words, too: *panacea* (see page 139), *pancreas* (literally "all flesh"), *pantechnicon, panorama.* Sadly, *panda, pangolin* and *pantyhose* are completely irrelevant here.

The root of the matter

Being aware of a few basics can help enormously with vocabulary and spelling, as the *bio-* and *pan-* examples show. Switching to Latin, for instance, *mater* and *pater* mean "mother" and "father," so that's a clue to the meaning of anything beginning with *matri-* or *patri-*: *patricide, patrimony, matriarch, matrilineal.**

Lux and its genitive form *lucis* mean "light," which helps with *lucid* and *elucidate.*

Vertere means "to turn," hence *vertigo, subvert, advertisement* (literally something you turn toward).

Intra means "within" and *inter* means "between," which explains the difference between the *Internet*, which is a link between various networks, and an *intranet*, which is confined to an individual company. Anything beginning with *pre-* has a good chance of meaning "before"; *post-* is likely to mean "after."

In *herbivore* and *carnivore*, the *-vore* is concerned with eating. So if you come across a *fructivorous* monkey or *sanguivorous* bat, you can at least be confident that you are being told about their diet, even if you aren't quite sure what it is they eat.

---

* *Matrimony* also comes from *mater* and has a complicated derivation that involves a no-longer-used meaning of "an inheritance from one's mother." *Patrimony*, however, still means "an inheritance from one's father" and has nothing to do with marriage.

Et cetera, et cetera, et cetera

Not only does half our language derive from Latin, but there are also still many Latin expressions in common use. Below are a few you'll come across most days of the week in perfectly unpretentious company.

It is worth noting that Latin didn't go in for silent letters in the way that English does, so you should pronounce every syllable. The exception is the *vice* in *vice versa*, which is now often a single syllable but would originally have been pronounced something like "wee-keh." In the Latin alphabet, the letter *v* could be used as either a vowel (when it served the same purpose as *u*) or a consonant (pronounced as *w*, which didn't exist as a separate letter until much later). Similarly, Latin had no *j*, but used *i* as a consonant in words such as *iustitia*, "justice," which would originally have been pronounced as if it began with a *y*. The same applies to other words associated with the law, such as *jury* and *adjudicate*, and also to words associated with youth such as *juvenile* and *junior*. And yes, clever dogs, you do sometimes see it spelled *IVSTITIA*.

ad hoc: literally "toward this," used to mean "for this special purpose" or "just to be going on with," as in "Heath Robinson made a number of ad hoc contraptions."

ad infinitum: "until infinity," usually in the sense of "and so on and so on."

ad lib: *ad libitum*, literally "according to pleasure." In other words, making it up as you go along, performing a play or giving a speech without sticking to the script, or indeed without having a script at all. Call it improv if you like.[*]

ad nauseam: "until nausea," usually in the sense of "and so on and so on until the listener is so bored they throw up."

alibi: literally "in another place." Originally an adverb, as in "The maid's evidence proved that the butler was alibi," now generally used as a noun: "The maid's evidence provided the butler with an alibi."

ars gratia artis: "art for art's sake." See the note about Corinthian columns on page 121, or find the song on *10CC's Greatest Hits.*

bona fide: literally "with good faith," usually used to mean "genuine," as in "a bona fide example of a Latin expression." Sometimes also a noun, meaning much the same as "credentials" (which comes from a Latin word meaning "to be believed"): "He presented his bona fides to the senior manager."

coitus interruptus: Oh, come on, you know what that means. But it does prove the point that Latin has some fairly basic uses. (Or, a cynic might say, that Latin is perhaps a bit outmoded after all.)

---

[*] *Libido*—also (some say) connected with pleasure—comes from the same root. Women's *lib*, which may not have anything to do with pleasure, is from a different source: It's short for *liberation* and is connected with *liberty* and *libertine*. *Librarians* and *Libras* are, as I'm sure you'll agree, another thing entirely.

cui bono: literally "for whose good?" Used in the more pretentious type of whodunit to establish who benefits from a crime and is therefore likely to have committed it. See *modus operandi*, below.

de facto: "in fact," or more explicitly "actual, though not officially recognized," as in "After Bill's resignation, Ben became the *de facto* chairman of the board." If Ben were later formally confirmed in the position, he would become the chairman *de jure*, "by law."

e.g.: *exempli gratia*, "for example," "e.g. this is an example." Not to be confused with *i.e.*, below.

et al.: *et alii*, "and other people." Used a couple of times in this book (see pages 109 and 134) to mean "and the rest of those guys."

etc.: *et cetera*: literally "and other things," widely used to mean "and so on."*

i.e.: *id est*, "that is," "i.e., not the same thing as *e.g.* and to be used when clarifying a statement rather than giving an example of it."

modus operandi: "way of working." Abbreviated as "MO" in detective fiction, it means that someone who goes around strangling people with silk scarves is unlikely to be the murderer of a victim who has been struck over the head with a poker.

---

* I think I am proving my point here. If it weren't for these Latin phrases, we would have to say "and so on" all the time, and that would be pretty dull.

N.B.: *nota bene*, literally "note well." "N.B. This abbreviation is not to be confused with *P.S.*, below."

non sequitur: "it doesn't follow." Originally a term from formal logic (see page 159, especially the bit about *post hoc propter hoc*), this is now used more widely to describe any statement that isn't relevant to what has gone before. As in "It was a non sequitur for Bill to claim that, having vacationed in Greece, he knew all about Aristotelian logic."

per annum: "each year," usually used to refer to salaries and sometimes abbreviated, as in '$100,000 p.a." Also, **per diem**, "each day," as in a consultant being paid a per diem rate of $10,000, or used as a noun, as in receiving a $100 per diem.

per capita: literally "by the heads," as in "the equivalent per capita expenditure was $7 a week."

per se: "in itself," as in "I don't need to win the lottery per se, but a sudden inheritance of half a million would come in rather handy."

pro rata: "in proportion," often applied to part-time jobs: "Three days a week, salary $25,000 pro rata" (meaning: salary appreciably less than $25,000).

P.S.: *post scriptum*, "after writing." Formerly used if you wanted to add something to a letter after you had signed it; nowadays more usually replaced by a second email headed "And here it is with the attachment this time." *Postscript* has also gone into the language as a noun denoting any afterthought or supplement, and if you put a capital *S* in the middle you get the name of what Wikipedia calls a "dynamically typed concatenative programming language." But of course you knew that already.

Q.E.D.: *quod erat demonstrandum,* "which was the thing that was supposed to be demonstrated," written (in the good old days, at least) at the end of a calculation in geometry, showing that you had worked out what you were supposed to have worked out. Also used more or less facetiously to mean "I've proven my point."

quid pro quo: "something for something," giving something in exchange or recompense for something else. Along the lines of "You scratch my back and I'll scratch yours" and not necessarily as vindictive as "tit for tat."

requiescat in pace: Never heard of it? Well, it abbreviates to *R.I.P.* and literally means "May he or she rest in peace." Most frequently seen on cartoon gravestones (and a few real ones) and Halloween decorations.

And lest you think that all Latin expressions are obsessed with money or death:

status quo: "the existing state of affairs," as in "If neither Johnny Depp nor George Clooney is available, I will have to put up with the status quo."

vice versa: "the other way round," as in "I could marry Johnny Depp and have an affair with George Clooney, or vice versa."

Less common but still around:

alea iacta est: "the die is cast." Allegedly said by Julius Caesar when he crossed the Rubicon (see page 83), it means "There's no going back now." Widely used in the *Asterix* books by Roman soldiers whenever something goes wrong.

carpe diem: "seize the day," so make the most of the opportunity, have fun, you may be dead tomorrow. From an ode by Horace (see page 114), whose philosophy of life this pretty much sums up.

caveat emptor: "let the buyer beware," meaning lift up the carpets and check for dampness, because it'll be your problem later.

de mortuis nil nisi bonum: "of the dead, nothing unless it is good," in other words: Don't speak ill of the dead.

in camera: literally "in the room,"* usually used in a legal sense of "behind closed doors," not in open court.

in situ: "in the original place," as in "The archaeologists could date the fossil because it was discovered *in situ.*"

in vino veritas: "in wine, truth." A nonsensical expression that suggests you tell the truth when you are drunk, when it should of course be "*in vino* gross exaggeration, distorted reality and maudlin self-pity."

---

* The modern word *chamber* derives from *camera*, as does, surprisingly enough, the modern word *camera*.

ipso facto: "by the fact itself," as in "An illegal immigrant, *ipso facto*, cannot be issued a passport."

res ipsa loquitur: "the thing speaks for itself," meaning "It's obvious, isn't it?" Briefly brought back from oblivion when British politician Boris Johnson used it as a justification for learning Latin.

sine qua non: "without which not," as in "Reliability is the *sine qua non* for success."

sub rosa: literally "under the rose," meaning "in secret," from the Roman habit of hanging a rose over a council table to indicate that all present were sworn to secrecy.

Singulars and plurals

Neither Latin nor Greek formed plurals by putting an *s* on the end of a word, which is one of the many reasons we have some irregular-looking words in English that not everyone recognizes as plurals.

Greek neuter words ending in *-on* had a plural form ending in *-a*, so *phenomenon* and *criterion* are singular, *phenomena* and *criteria* are plural.

Latin neuter words ending in *-um* also end in *-a* in the plural, leaving us with *medium/media, datum/data, bacterium/ bacteria.*

Latin feminine nouns ending in *-a* have *-ae* in the plural; not common in modern English, but *formula/formulae* is one example; masculine nouns ending in *-us* are pluralized as *-i*: *alumnus/alumni* and, come to think of it, if they are women, *alumna/alumnae.*

Some Latin nouns ending in *-is* changed to *-es* for the plural: *crisis/crises, thesis/theses.*

And then there are some oddities (which were perfectly regular in Latin): *opus/opera, genus/genera, index/indices, matrix/matrices, species/species.*

Speaking of genera and species

Another common use of Latin in English (as it were) is in the "technical" naming of plants and animals. An eighteenth-century Swede named Linnaeus developed what we now call **taxonomy**, which means that he classified all the known plants and animals into genera and species (and orders and all sorts of other things that are outside the scope of this book). Many of his names were descriptive, so that if you come across a plant whose name has *folia* or *folium* in it, you know that it is talking about the leaves (think *foliage*), and if it has *aurea* or *aureus,* it is golden. *Rosa canina* is the dog rose (think about it), and *Helleborus foetidus* is the stinking hellebore.

And finally...

Throughout history we have had to invent new words for new things or new concepts, and not everyone is as well informed about Latin and Greek as they used to be. Hence *television* (literally "far seeing") is a confusion of a Greek beginning and a Latin ending; and that once widely used word *psychedelic* is what the *Oxford Dictionary* describes as "irregularly formed": If it had been coined by a classical scholar, it would have been *psychodelic*.

2

The Made-Up Stuff: Religion and Mythology

The **Greek gods** were a complicated lot, partly because there were so many of them, partly because of their penchant for incest, and partly because there are a number of conflicting stories about their origins and activities. The bible—for lack of a better word—on the subject is Hesiod's *Theogony*, a poem composed in around 700 B.C., but Homer, Ovid and Uncle Tom Cobley have their own variations. So don't write in, OK?

Each god was responsible for his or her own area of expertise, so the Greeks would seek support from Aphrodite in matters of love, or make sure Poseidon was in a good mood before going on a sea voyage. Priests were on hand to conduct sacrifices on holy days, or check the omens to see whether a certain day would be auspicious for a particular journey or marriage, but there wasn't the modern concept of "going to church." For the most part, the humble mortal could go along to the relevant temple with his gift of wine or honey, or a piglet, and offer it to the god on his own account. Some gods required an animal to be sacrificed, while others could be mollified with a few plumes of smoke, leaving the sacrificial meat for the humans to eat.

The gods' family tree

In the beginning, reasonably enough, there was a state of nothingness known as **Chaos**, from which was born **Gaia** (Earth, also spelled Gaea, Ge and sundry other ways). She produced a son, **Uranus** (heaven), who also became the father of her children. If this shocks you, you might like to skip the rest of this section.

The children concerned were a whole horde of giants, including two **Titans** named Oceanus and Tethys, whom Homer calls the progenitors of the gods. Hesiod, however, suggests that Uranus was overthrown by another Titan son, **Cronus**, who in turn was overthrown by his own son, **Zeus**. There are lots of contradictory accounts involving castration and the swallowing of their own children, but we haven't got room for that here.

Some versions of the story have Zeus drawing lots with his brothers **Poseidon** and **Hades**, but however it happened Zeus became king of the gods and married **Hera**, who was also his sister. They lived on **Mount Olympus**, where they did wonders for property prices, luring all the major gods to the neighborhood. Tradition has it that there were twelve "Olympian" gods, though not always the same twelve. In due course, the Romans adopted them all and gave them new Latin names, shown in parentheses here:

Zeus (**Jupiter** or **Jove**), lord of the skies, was prone to throwing thunderbolts at anyone who displeased him, and to changing himself into a variety of forms in order to have sex with anything that moved. He turned into a swan to seduce Leda, fathering Helen of Troy and the twins Castor and Pollux (now better known as the constellation of Gemini); into a bull with Europa, who gave birth to Minos, king of Crete (see page 41); and into a shower of gold to impress Danaë, who was suitably dazzled and gave birth to Perseus (see page 47). He also had affairs with Semele, producing Dionysus (Bacchus), the god of wine; with Maia (see *Hermes*, page 34) and many more. Zeus's legitimate offspring with Hera included Hephaestus and Ares (see page 29), and Athena sprang fully armed from his head—or at least that's what Zeus told Hera when he came home after a particularly heavy night and spent the next day groping for Tylenol.

Poseidon (**Neptune**) came second in the lot-drawing contest and got to be god of the sea. Notoriously short-tempered, he wrought havoc if anyone offended him, using a trident that could shake the earth. Appeasing the temperamental gods was always a good move, and staying on the right side of Poseidon was vital for anyone thinking of setting foot on a boat. The bearded version of Neptune who still appears on ships crossing the equator is a much jollier character.

Pluto or **Hades** (**Dis**) drew the shortest straw and became god of the Underworld (the place itself is also called Hades). He fell in love with Persephone (Proserpina), daughter of Demeter (Ceres), the goddess of corn and agriculture,* and abducted her to live in the Underworld with him. Demeter neglected her agricultural duties while searching for her daughter and the earth became barren. Eventually Pluto agreed to let Persephone spend six months of the year above ground, as long as she spent the other six months in the Underworld with him. Demeter remained in mourning while her daughter was absent—thus creating autumn and winter—but returned to the daily grind during the other two seasons.

Although he was king of the Underworld, Pluto wasn't a devil. There are plenty of bad guys kicking around in classical mythology (and some pretty mean women too), but no equivalent of Satan or Lucifer. That said, people certainly suffered in Hades. There's Tantalus, for example, doomed to perpetual hunger and thirst because the water he stood in receded whenever he bent down to drink, and the fruit above his head remained—wait for it—*tantalizingly* out of his reach. But the Elysian Fields, the nearest classical mortals got to what we might call Heaven, were also in the Underworld. There's more about all this in the box on page 30.

Hera (**Juno**) was the goddess of marriage and a particular protector of married women. Zeus's chronic infidelity meant that jealousy and strife were commonplace in stories featuring

---

* …and namesake of corn-based breakfast *cereal*, from Cocoa Puffs to Corn Pops.

Hera. And when she became angry at someone, she stayed angry at them and could be pretty drastic: See, for example, the Labors of Hercules (page 39), although that is far from being the only time she let her temper get the better of her.

Hestia (**Vesta**) was the sister of Zeus and Hera, and goddess of the hearth. A rather homely figure, she was a virgin goddess, perhaps to make up for the total lack of chastity among some of her peers. Vesta is unusual among Roman goddesses in that her worship was not influenced by her Greek counterpart: In Roman times, she was the patron of the Vestal Virgins, priestesses whose virtue was inviolable—they were buried alive if they were caught with a man in their room—and whose duties included guarding the sacred fire that was never allowed to go out.

Ares (**Mars**) was the son of Zeus and Hera, and the god of war. Interestingly enough, more of a problem child than a dignified deity—he liked to stir up trouble but frequently behaved in a cowardly and unchivalrous way. When Hephaestus discovered him with Aphrodite (see page 33), he caught the two of them up in a net and exposed them to the ridicule of the other gods. The Roman figure was a little more respectable: The Campus Martius, scene of great chariot races, was dedicated to Mars, and the word *martial* (as in "martial law") derives from his name.

Athena (**Minerva**), the one who was born in that rather unconventional way (see *Zeus*, page 27), was the goddess of war and of wisdom, with a particular interest in Athens. Her

(continued on page 32)

About the Underworld

The **Underworld**—sometimes called Hades, sometimes Avernus—appears in so many myths and legends that it deserves a box to itself. The best description of it comes in Book VI of the *Aeneid* (see *Virgil*, page 113), when Aeneas is escorted by an ancient prophetess called the Sibyl to visit his father, Anchises, and see evidence of the future glories of Rome. Virgil puts the entrance to the Underworld somewhere near Mount Vesuvius and says, in the (loosely translated) words of the Sibyl, "The descent to Avernus is not hard. It's getting back that's tricky."

To get into the Underworld you had to be rowed across the **River Styx** by the boatman **Charon**, who charged a fee, which explains why corpses were buried with a coin in their mouths. You also had to get past **Cerberus**, the three-headed dog, which the Sibyl did by throwing him a drugged cake she had prepared earlier. Other rivers of the Underworld included the **Acheron** and the **Cocytus**, which were just black and swirly and nasty, and the **Lethe**, the Underworld's solution to overcrowding. This could be a problem even in those days, so, after a thousand years, souls down below were allowed to take on another body and go back up to Earth as someone else; drinking the waters of the Lethe made them forget everything that had gone before.

At the entrance to the Underworld, the road divided, leading you either to Hell (**Tartarus**) or to Heaven (**Elysium** or the **Elysian Fields**). Tartarus was pretty grim. It had a burning river called the **Phlegethon**, and **Tisiphone**, one of the Furies (see page 36), spent her time whipping the inmates and threatening them with snakes. Elysium, on the other hand, let you play music and dance or whatever else had turned you on when you were alive.

The very few people who weren't dead managed, for various reasons, to get down to the Underworld and back. They included:

• **Hercules** (see page 39)

• **Theseus**, whose mate Pirithous lusted after Persephone. The two of them were caught by Pluto, but Hercules eventually liberated Theseus, leaving Pirithous to his fate.

• **Orpheus**, the great musician, whose wife **Eurydice** had died. Orpheus was grief-stricken and wheedled his way into the Underworld to beg for her return. His heart softened by Orpheus's music, Pluto agreed, on condition that Orpheus did not look back at Eurydice "until they had reached the upper air." Alas, Orpheus couldn't resist the temptation, and Eurydice was drawn back into the Underworld for good. Orpheus himself was killed shortly afterward and thus reunited with his wife. His lyre was placed in the heavens as the constellation Lyra, and a nightingale is said to sing more sweetly over his grave than anywhere else. Orpheus's story has inspired many great musical works, including what some consider the first opera, by Monteverdi.

symbol was the owl, which remains the symbol of the city to this day. She is also known as Pallas Athena.

Apollo (**Apollo**) was the son of Zeus and Leto, a minor goddess in her own right. When she became pregnant, Leto had to travel the world looking for somewhere to give birth, since everyone was terrified of incurring Hera's wrath if they let her in. Eventually she found refuge on the tiny island of Delos, which has remained sacred to Apollo ever afterward. He was the god of, among other things, music and of light: Every morning he harnessed his chariot and drove the sun across the sky (in this context he is also known as Phoebus Apollo, or just Phoebus).

Apollo inherited his father's libertine tendencies and spent a lot of his time pursuing nymphs: Daphne's father turned her into the tree that bears her name so that she could avoid his advances, which is why Apollo is often depicted wearing a laurel crown (the daphne being a member of the laurel family, for the non-gardeners among you). He also took a shine to Cassandra, daughter of Priam, King of Troy, and granted her the gift of prophecy; when they had a tiff, he added the curse that no one would believe anything she said. She, poor lass, later wandered around the ruins of Troy muttering, "I told you so. Don't take in that horse, I said. But would anybody listen? Oh, no." But of course nobody paid any attention.

The **Oracle at Delphi**, famous for its unhelpful, ambiguous predictions, but also for giving the ancient Greeks advice on political matters, was sacred to Apollo.

Artemis (**Diana**) was the twin sister of Apollo, and goddess of hunting and the moon. Another virgin. The story goes that the hunter Actaeon came upon her when she was bathing; she was so outraged that she turned him into a stag and he was torn apart by his own hounds. Two paintings by Titian depict this story, and it is interesting to note that, even in the second one when she has had time to get dressed, pick up her bow and arrows and lace up a complicated pair of sandals, the modest maiden still has a breast hanging out of her dress.

Aphrodite (**Venus**) was the goddess of love and beauty. There was nothing virginal about her, and some unpleasant diseases are named after her. Some say she was the daughter of Zeus and Dione,* others that she rose from the sea on a scallop shell, as in the painting by Botticelli. Aphrodite was married to her brother Hephaestus (see page 27) but had an affair with her brother Ares. She also fell in love with a particularly beautiful youth called Adonis (no relation), who was later killed while out hunting. There's a long poem by Shakespeare about this.

Aphrodite's son **Eros** (**Cupid**) is generally portrayed as a chubby baby who mischievously shoots arrows at people to make them fall in love, usually with someone who couldn't be less interested. Contrary to popular belief, the statue in London's Piccadilly Circus that celebrates the work of the Victorian philanthropist Lord Shaftesbury doesn't depict Eros at all; it's his brother,

---

* The sources are vague about who Dione was. She may have risen from the sea.

Anteros, who represents requited, rational love. But as they looked rather similar, it's a mistake anyone could have made.

And speaking of words derived from the names of gods, we can add *erotic* and *cupidinous* here—neither of them closely associated with Victorian philanthropy.

Hermes (**Mercury**) was the son of Zeus and Maia, daughter of Atlas (see page 44). Hermes was the messenger of the gods and got around with the help of a winged helmet and winged sandals; he also carried a rod entwined with two serpents known as the caduceus. Famous for his cunning, he was the god of wealth and presided over both merchants and thieves.

Hephaestus (**Vulcan**), son of Zeus and Hera (or, if you believe Hesiod, Hera alone), was the god of fire, and the blacksmith and armorer of the gods. His forge sat under Mount Etna in Sicily. An ugly baby, he was banished from Heaven either by Hera because she couldn't stand the sight of him or by Zeus for taking Hera's side in a quarrel between the two (as I have mentioned, there was never any shortage of those). Hephaestus may have been born lame or broken his legs as he fell from Olympus. Either way, he ended up crippled as well as ugly, but was given the beautiful Aphrodite as his wife as a reward for forging Zeus's thunderbolts. Unsurprisingly, it turned out not to be a marriage made in Heaven (see various references to her infidelities, above, never mind the fact that she was his sister).

These are the principal gods of Olympus, although there was occasional to-ing and fro-ing. Some say that Hestia went to live among mortals and gave up her place to Dionysus; others mention that Pluto actually lived in the Underworld, so there was a spare room, sometimes occupied by Demeter.

There are many other **demigods**, **heroes**, **nymphs** and what have you (as you might expect with all that fooling around going on); the most important of them turn up when the mood takes them in various parts of this book.

The female of the species

In addition to the main gods, there are several groups of women—goddesses, primeval beings, call them what you will—who crop up again and again in the myths and can be confusing. And there are times when it is important to know the difference between a goddess who will inspire you to write beautiful poetry and one who will turn you to stone if you so much as look at her.

The Nine Muses

More daughters of Zeus: Their mother was Mnemosyne, another Titan and the goddess of memory.* The Muses lived on **Mount Parnassus** and inspired musicians and artists. They were:

• **Calliope:** the muse of epic or heroic poetry
• **Clio:** the muse of history

---

* Hence *mnemonic* devices.

- **Erato:** the muse of lyric and love poetry*
- **Euterpe:** the muse of music
- **Melpomene:** the muse of tragedy
- **Polymnia:** the muse of sacred song
- **Terpsichore:** the muse of dance
- **Thalia:** the muse of comedy
- **Urania:** the muse of astronomy

The Three Fates or *Moirae* (*Parcae* in Latin)

Controlled the lifespan of mortals and immortals alike:

- **Clotho** spun the thread of life from her distaff
- **Lachesis** assigned and measured each lifespan's length
- **Atropos** cut it and therefore decided when and how mortals died

The Three Furies or *Erinyes*

The personifications of vengeance: **Alecto**, **Megaera** and **Tisiphone**. They were particularly hot on crimes against the ties of kinship, which is why they pursued Orestes so violently after he had killed his mother, Clytemnestra. (You may think they had a point, but he got off in the end—see page 105.) Aeschylus's *Oresteia* calls these ladies the Eumenides or "Gracious Ones," but this is probably just a feeble attempt to appease a group of angry crones surrounded by snakes.

---

* A word much beloved of crossword puzzlers. It is the only possible answer to the entry e_a_o, which appears surprisingly often.

The Gorgons

Another group of angry crones, the most famous of whom was **Medusa**. They had serpents in their hair and girdles, and anyone who met their gaze was turned to stone. Medusa was killed by Perseus, who chopped off her head while she was sleeping, having avoided looking directly at her by using her reflection in the shiny shield he had been given by Hermes. Which, when you think about it, is pretty darned clever, and would have taken quite a bit of practice in front of the bathroom mirror. Medusa was pregnant by Poseidon at the time and the winged horse Pegasus sprang from her blood.

The great thing about being a Gorgon was that you retained the ability to turn people to stone even after you had died and had your head cut off. How cool is that?

The Harpies

In Homer and Hesiod these were violent winds that carried people away to their deaths. By the time of Virgil, they had turned into birds with the faces of women, but the effect was the same.

During the Middle Ages, there were continued literary references to harpies. In his *Inferno*, Dante envisages the tortured wood infested with harpies, where the suicides have their punishment in the second ring.

The Sirens

At last, some halfway decent-looking women! The problem with the Sirens, though, was that they sang in a hypnotic way that lured seafaring men to their deaths on the rocks. Orpheus, passing near them, played beautifully on his lyre to drown them out; Odysseus protected his men by stuffing their ears with wax, which, according to one version of the story, caused the Sirens to drown themselves in a (rather drastic) fit of pique.

Scylla and Charybdis

Scylla was a (female, of course) sea monster who seized and devoured sailors who passed too close to her cave; Charybdis dragged them into a whirlpool nearby, so the two made for a particularly tough navigational challenge. Odysseus, who was a bit of a smartass, survived them, as did Jason and the Argonauts. Tradition has it that Scylla and Charybdis are in the Straits of Messina, between Sicily and Italy, where a natural whirlpool makes sailing tricky to this day. The expression "between Scylla and Charybdis" is still sometimes used to mean much the same as "between the Devil and the deep blue sea," that is, stuck with the choice of two unattractive options, or "between a rock and a hard place," given that Scylla's cave was cut out of a rock.

The Labors of Hercules

So after gods and monsters come superheroes, and other bits and pieces of mythology that have lingered on in our culture and vocabulary. People still talk about a Herculean task, which might mean as little as cleaning up after a dinner party. The original twelve Labors of Hercules were rather tougher.

Hercules is the Roman name for the Greek Heracles, and I'm using the Roman form here because it's more familiar to most of us, but either way he was a great hero, known for his strength, courage and hearty appetite (for all sorts of things). He was a son of Zeus by Alcmene, daughter of the King of Mycenae, and—in common with many of Zeus's other out-of-wedlock offspring—was persecuted by Hera; indeed, she sent a load of serpents to kill him in his cradle, but he strangled them effortlessly, which pretty much set the pattern for the rest of his life.

Thanks to Hera, Hercules was later overcome by a fit of madness and murdered his wife and children; when he asked the Oracle at Delphi how he could purify himself of this crime, he was told to go to Tiryns and serve King Eurystheus, who happened to be his worst enemy and could be guaranteed to give him a hard time. It was Eurystheus who imposed the Labors. As is so often the case, sources and details vary, but the usual list is:

To kill the Nemean Lion. This lion was such a fearful thing that a club wasn't good enough, so Hercules strangled it, skinned it and thereafter wore the skin as a mantle— scaring Eurystheus half to death when he went back to Tiryns to report success.

To kill the Lernaean Hydra. The Hydra was a monster with many heads, each of which regrew whenever cut off. Hercules enlisted the help of his friend Iolaus, who sealed the stumps with a "burning brand" as Hercules cut off each head. (Some sources report that there were nine heads, only one of them immortal, and Hercules ended up burying that one under a rock.)

To capture the Hind of Ceryneia. This was a deer with golden horns, sacred to Artemis, so Eurystheus included it specifically to get Hercules into trouble with the goddess. Hercules chased it for a year before running it down.

To capture the Erymanthian Boar. He tired it out by driving it through a snowdrift, and then caught it in a net. Erymanthos is a mountain, so relying on a snowdrift in Greece is not as silly as it sounds.

To clean out the Augean Stables. Sounds easy enough, but the problem here was that there were a lot of cattle, the stables hadn't been mucked out for thirty years, and Hercules had only one day to do the cleaning (which seems mean given that he was allowed to spend a whole year chasing a hind). He diverted a couple of rivers and flushed the stables out.

To get rid of the Stymphalian Birds. These were allegedly man-eating monsters, and Hercules scared them from their coverts using a brass rattle and either shot them or drove them away.

To capture the Cretan Bull, probably the one that had fathered the Minotaur (see page 52). The bull was rampaging all over Crete, so Minos was perfectly happy for Hercules to take it. He released it in Mycenae, where it carried on rampaging, finally settling near Marathon and eventually being killed by Theseus.

To tame the Horses of Diomedes, because they were fed with human flesh. Hercules killed Diomedes and fed his flesh to the horses, which seems to have turned them off the whole carnivore thing.

To capture the Girdle of Hippolyta, Queen of the Amazons, because Eurystheus's daughter wanted it. Hippolyta was going to be nice about it (hey, she was a queen, she probably had other girdles), but Hera persuaded the rest of the Amazons that Hippolyta was being abducted and the whole thing degenerated into the sort of battle you see on the opening day of the December 26th sales.

To capture the Oxen of Geryon. This involved going to the very western edge of the known world, where the Pillars of Hercules (on either side of the Strait of Gibraltar) mark the spot. Hercules accomplished the journey by forcing the sun god Helios to give up the golden bowl that carried him back to the east at the end of every day. Hercules then killed Geryon, captured the cattle and brought them home in the golden bowl. These cattle ate human flesh, too, but presumably Hercules had figured that one out by this time.

To capture the Apples of the Hesperides. These golden apples had been given to Hera on her wedding day, and the Hesperides were the girls who guarded them. The problem was that Hercules didn't know where they were. He got around this with a trick: either conning a sea deity called Nereus into telling him where the gardens were, or conning Atlas, who was father to the Hesperides, into getting the apples for him.

To capture Cerberus, the three-headed dog who guarded the Underworld (see page 30). Hercules descended to the Underworld with the help of Hermes and Athena (both of whom Hera hated, so we are in the realms of "my enemy's enemy is my friend" here), overpowered the dog with brute strength, took him to Eurystheus to show that he could do it, and then took him home again.

The Judgment of Paris

This was one of the most important decisions in all mythology. There's a lesson to be learned from this story: Invite people to parties; they'll be offended if you don't.

Eris, the goddess of Discord, was the only one of the gang not invited to the wedding of Peleus and Thetis (don't worry about who they are—they're just the ones around whom the action happens). Hanging around outside, she threw a golden apple among the guests, inscribed "For the fairest." Hera, Athena and Aphrodite all made a grab for it and then called on Zeus to arbitrate. Well, you know what it's like at weddings—everyone's a tad overwrought, one wrong word and *someone*'s going to end up in tears—so Zeus wisely passed the buck to Paris.

Remember that these are gods we are dealing with. They're used to getting their own way, and bribing the judge is all in a day's work. Hera offered Paris power and wealth if he chose her, Athena promised that he would win glory in war, and Aphrodite suggested he might like to marry the most beautiful woman in the world.

No prizes for guessing which he chose.

The most beautiful woman in the world was **Helen**, who was married to **Menelaus**, King of Sparta. Not allowing this detail to stand in his way, Paris invited himself to stay and, with the help of Aphrodite, persuaded Helen to elope with him to **Troy**. Where very soon they found there was a war on, with Hera and Athena firmly on the other side. Remember I mentioned that when Hera got mad she stayed mad? Well, this war lasted ten years and she didn't let up.

Turn to page 101 for Homer's version of the rest of the story. And if you are getting married in the near future, be careful with your guest list.

Miscellaneous myths

I've included some famous mythological figures in the chapter on literature (see page 101), but here are a few more that might otherwise have slipped through the net:

Atlas: A son of one of the Titans, and involved in their revolt against the gods of Olympus. As punishment he was condemned to hold up the pillars separating heaven and earth. This image frequently appeared as the frontispiece of books of maps in the sixteenth century, which is why they are "atlases" now, not "books of maps." Atlas was inhospitable to Perseus (see page 47), who used the head of Medusa to turn him into a mountain range in North Africa, which takes almost as much talent as cutting someone's head off while looking at their reflection in a shield, and makes me think that Perseus could have taught David Copperfield a thing or two.

Jason and the Argonauts: Stop me if you've heard this one, but there was this ram with a golden fleece. Oh, there just was, OK? The ram was sacrificed to Zeus, and its fleece hung up in a place called Colchis, over to the east of the Black Sea (absolutely the back end of beyond, in mythological terms).

For reasons too complicated to explain, it became Jason's task to get it back. He set off with fifty other heroes on a ship called the *Argo*, so the men aboard it were the Argonauts.

You could have written an *Odyssey* about the adventures they had on the way, only somehow a *Jasony* doesn't have the same ring to it. Once they got to Colchis, though, the king agreed to hand over the fleece as long as Jason performed a number of ludicrous tasks. These included yoking to a plow a pair of fire-breathing oxen with brass feet and sowing the teeth of a dragon, from which would spring armed men who would turn on the sower. The king's daughter, Medea, who conveniently happened a) to be a sorceress, and b) to have fallen in love with Jason, helped him to do all these things, and also to dope the dragon that guarded the fleece. So, mission accomplished, the Argonauts set off for home, with Medea tagging along because Jason had promised to marry her. Yeah, that old line. For Euripides's version of what happened next, see page 107, and to see how this became useful in philosophy, see page 154.

Midas: King of Phrygia, who was granted a wish by Silenus, a companion of Dionysus. Midas wished that everything he touched would turn to gold, not realizing that this would include his food, the water he tried to wash in and, in some versions, his daughter. When he explained very quietly and reasonably to Dionysus that he hadn't really meant it, the god sent him to wash in the River Pactolus, and Midas went back to normal. A later king of the area, Croesus, became proverbially rich because he could mint money (literally by the bucketload) from the gold dust in the river. It's sort of true, too: Croesus is the only person in this section who probably existed, and there are deposits of gold in the bed of the Pactolus to this day. Despite this cautionary tale, to have "the Midas touch," meaning to find it easy to make money, is generally considered a good thing.

The other story about Midas is that he was called upon to judge between the music of Pan and Apollo and found in favor of Pan. Apollo, understandably annoyed (he was, after all, god of music, whereas Pan was merely god of shepherds and tootled on the occasional pipe in his spare time), punished Midas by making a pair of ass's ears sprout from his head.

Pandora: The first woman, created by Hephaestus at Zeus's instruction and endowed by the gods with "all the gifts" (that's what her name means). The idea, according to one version of the story, was to punish both Prometheus for stealing fire from Heaven (see next page) and man for accepting the gift. Another version says that Pandora (that is, woman) was sent by Zeus as a blessing to man, so you can believe whichever you prefer, according to your gender, marital status and frame of mind. Either way, she had been given a mysterious box and told by Zeus never to open it. When she inevitably did open it, she released all the evils that have since afflicted the world, from rheumatism and colic to spitefulness and jealousy. Only hope was left behind. The moral of the story being that, whatever sorrows may afflict us, hope is always there to provide comfort. Sweet.

Perseus: Had a head start on some of the other heroes because he was the son of Zeus, which is a bit like being Superman without having to worry about kryptonite. His big task was to kill Medusa, one of the Gorgons (see page 37). That done, he was flying around using Hermes's winged shoes, when he came upon Andromeda chained to a rock and about to be devoured by a sea serpent. He was able to stab the serpent, rescue the girl and marry her. Then, after one of those laughable misunderstandings that are all too common in mythology, he killed his grandfather* and took himself off into exile in Asia, where his not-very-imaginatively-named son Perses became the first king of the not-very-imaginatively-named Persians.

---

* With chilling parallels to the story of Oedipus (see page 106), there had been a prophecy when Perseus was born that he would kill his grandfather, and the old man thought he could get around it by sending the baby away. A word of warning: When you are a character in mythology and you try to stop a prophecy from coming true, *it never works.*

Prometheus: One of the Titans, whose name means "forethought." With his brother Epimetheus ("afterthought") he was given the task of creating man, and giving him and the animals all the qualities that they would need in order to survive. Epimetheus was so generous, handing out wisdom to the owl, strength to the lion, a hard shell to the tortoise and so on, that when he came to man, who was supposed to be superior to the rest, he had nothing left to give. At his instigation and with the help of Athena, Prometheus went up to heaven, lit his torch from the heat of the sun and brought fire down to earth for the first time. This was the gift that made humans able to produce tools that would till the land, make weapons, keep themselves warm in winter, and a number of other things with which the animals couldn't compete. Zeus wasn't very pleased with this presumptuousness and had Prometheus chained to a rock where an eagle perpetually pecked at his liver, which grew again every night.

Pygmalion: Sculpted a statue of a woman so beautiful that he fell in love with her. In answer to his prayers, Aphrodite brought the statue to life, Pygmalion married the woman he had created and, according to Ovid, they lived happily ever after.

Before this happened, though, Pygmalion spent a lot of time admiring the brilliance of his own work, much like Professor Higgins in Shaw's play but with more actual groping. In Shaw's version, first performed in 1913, the only references to the legend are in the preface and postscript, not in the text itself—he presumably expected his audience to know what the title meant. By the 1950s, this would no longer have been a safe assumption, and so *My Fair Lady* was born.

Galatea, the name of the statue, was popularized by W. S. Gilbert (of Gilbert and Sullivan fame), who wrote a comedy on the subject; it doesn't appear in the early sources.

3

A Detour: Crete

This section goes much further back in time than most of the Greek history covered in the next chapter, but there are two reasons for that:

- You can't ignore Crete just because it doesn't fit in with the time frame.

- It provides a useful link between mythology and history. Yes, it has improbable stuff about Minotaurs and labyrinths and balls of thread, but the fact that you can still visit the ruins of the **Palace of Knossos** suggests that there are some elements of truth to the story. Rather like Croesus and the river full of gold dust (see page 46), it can't *all* have been made up by bards to wile away a long winter's evening.

It seems to be pretty certain that there was a settlement in Crete as early as 6000 B.C., and the **Minoan** civilization—named after a great king, or possibly a number of kings, called **Minos**—flourished until about 1500 B.C., most probably destroyed by a volcanic eruption and/or an earthquake. The palace once had glorious frescoes showing the bull-leaping to which the Cretans were prone (see overleaf), but most of what remains of these is now in the Archaeological Museum in the capital, **Heraklion**.

More than one expert describes the ruins of Knossos as labyrinthine, so it's not unreasonable to imagine that there was once a labyrinth here—and that's where myths become intertwined with history.

The story goes that Poseidon had given King Minos a bull, which Minos then refused to sacrifice to him. In punishment, Poseidon caused Minos's wife **Pasiphaë** to fall in love with the bull and give birth to the **Minotaur**, a creature that was part-man, part-bull.[*] Bulls were quite the thing in those days—the Minoans practised bull-leaping and bull sacrifice, and archaeologists have found remnants of bull masks and bull horns. But interestingly, Minos wasn't best pleased to be saddled with the bastard offspring of his wife and her taurine paramour.

In order to keep the Minotaur under control, Minos got the master craftsman **Daedalus** to construct a maze or labyrinth for the creature to live in. Every year the Minotaur was fed the seven youths and seven maidens that Minos demanded from Athens as an annual tribute. (They did that sort of thing in those days, and you can imagine that a Minotaur might

---

[*] See page 25 for advice on not annoying Poseidon.

have a hearty appetite.*) Anyway, **Theseus**, an Athenian hero, determined to put a stop to this shocking waste of Athenian youth, came to Knossos to destroy the Minotaur. Minos's daughter **Ariadne** fell in love with him and provided him with a ball of thread so that he could find his way out of the labyrinth.

Monster destroyed, ritual sacrifice abolished, hero and heroine united – end of story, you might have thought. Unfortunately, Theseus got tired of Ariadne and abandoned her on the island of Naxos, where she became the subject of an opera by Richard Strauss. She was subsequently taken up by the god **Dionysus,** the Greek equivalent of Bacchus, the god of wine. So presumably she lived happily ever after, unless bacchanalian orgies were not to her taste.

There are lots of other vaguely familiar legends tacked on to this story, so let's get them out of the way while we remember:

- When Minos died he became one of the judges of the Underworld, and assigned the dead to the afterlife task of his choice (see page 51 for more about the options he had there).

- Daedalus was later imprisoned in the labyrinth himself and, being the clever craftsman he was, made wings for himself

---

* Come to think of it, the Minotaur is another example of a creature you might have expected to be an herbivore preferring to eat human flesh—see the Labors of Hercules on page 39. Clearly the four stomachs of the ruminants still had some evolving to do.

and his son **Icarus**[*] so that they could escape. Icarus, getting above himself in more senses than one, flew so close to the sun that the wax on his wings melted and he fell into the sea and drowned.

• Theseus already had a son, **Hippolytus**, by the Amazon queen **Hippolyta** (the one who had the girdle that Hercules needed to steal; see page 41). Having abandoned Ariadne, Theseus then got involved with her sister **Phaedra**, who promptly fell in love with Hippolytus, a virtuous youth who rejected her advances. Lots of lies and denouncing and curses followed (at least they did in the play by Racine that you may have done for French 101), with the result that both Phaedra and Hippolytus were killed, and Theseus was left to ponder whether chastity might not be the answer from now on.

---

[*] From the wax and feathers that just happened to be lying around in the labyrinth, you understand.

4

The Old Stuff I:
Ancient Greek History

It's difficult to know with a book such as this precisely how far back in time to go. The Persian Wars, for example, are an important part of the history of Athens, but the entry for Persian Wars in *The Oxford Companion to Classical Literature* begins "The Assyrian empire had collapsed with the fall of Nineveh in 606 B.C., and had been followed by the Median empire under Cyaxares and Astyages." To me that single sentence raises five questions beginning with the words *who*, *what* and *where*, so I think I had better just jump into the middle somewhere.

By about the ninth century B.C., the ancient Greeks spoke mutually comprehensible dialects and worshipped the same gods, but politically the area we now call Greece was divided into **city-** or **citizen-states** (*poleis*, singular *polis* as in *metropolis*). These were ruled by kings and later by aristocratic families (*aristo-* means "the best"), who served as both magistrates and priests.

Although in these early days there were other important city-states—Corinth was one—**Athens** soon emerged at the top of the heap. Legend associates the founding of the city with Theseus (see page 53), who may or may not have existed, but certainly most of the great Greek dramatists and philosophers came from or worked in Athens, as did a couple of famous orators and politicians. Oh, and the Athenians invented democracy.

Aha! That might be the place to start.

The birth of democracy

As time went on, the dominance of the aristocratic clans lessened and they tended to be replaced by individual monarch-style rulers whom the Greeks called **tyrants**. The word didn't have quite the negative overtones that it does in modern English, but it still wasn't a compliment. Power continued to be inherited by sons who weren't always up to the job; at the same time increased trading produced a handful of wealthy merchants whose lack of important relatives disqualified them from public office.

Disaster waiting to happen, you say?

Well, not really, because the Athenians were basically a rational people who preferred to solve their problems through the rule of law rather than revolution if they could. But there was a certain amount of unrest.

The first famous figure to emerge from this was **Draco**, who has given his name to very harsh measures in any context, as well as to a character in *Harry Potter* who provokes the audience to hiss whenever he appears. The original Draco amended the laws of Athens so that crimes were no longer punished by private vengeance (believe it or not, the norm up until then) but by a system of public justice, establishing tribunals a bit like a modern judicial court. This may not sound all that draconian, but Draco did make liberal use of the death penalty, if that isn't a contradiction in terms. What I mean is, you could be executed for almost anything. Within thirty years another important politician, **Solon**, had come along and repealed almost all of Draco's laws.

Solon has gone down in history as "the law-giver" and, although he wasn't the only one by any means, he is generally considered to have been the wisest. One of his great concerns was the freedom of the Athenian people. Up until his time (he became chief magistrate in 594 B.C.), one Athenian citizen could enslave another who owed him money; Solon made this illegal and instituted a system whereby any citizen could seek justice from any other, regardless of the status or wealth of the individuals concerned. For the first time, wealth rather than class became a qualification for public office.

It's an interesting insight into the Athenian mindset that both Draco and Solon were aristocrats, so they were cleaning up the system from the inside. They also marked a firm departure from the notion that law-givers were divinely inspired—the priestesses of the Oracle at Delphi had previously been known to accept the occasional bribe in order to give the answer that a tyrant wanted.

These two also paved the way for a guy named **Cleisthenes** to go one step further.

Now here's another interesting thing. At the time we're talking about (508 B.C., if you're taking notes), this man was a highly regarded elder statesman in Athens, so he had been around for a while and done other stuff; he then made a speech that changed the course of world politics forever—and I'd never heard of him until I started work on this book. Why isn't he as famous as Socrates or the Magna Carta? Did he die in vain?

Not really. What happened was that he stood up in a public meeting and said, "I know. Let's give power to the people."

It was, almost, as simple as that. There had been troubles in the preceding couple of years, Solon's constitution was not working as well as it had been, and the Athenians needed to be rid of aristocratic and tyrannical rule once and for all. What Cleisthenes introduced was a system based not on family groups but on what we might now call parishes; he called them **demes**, a word derived from *demos*, meaning "the populace." Every male citizen over the age of thirty could register with his local deme. To supplement the existing Senate, Solon had created a "lower house" or council, which sometimes opened discussion to a larger public assembly, the

Ecclesia; under Cleisthenes, membership of the council was opened to all, and more important, the Ecclesia—and therefore every male citizen over thirty—was given a say in every major public decision. And each man, regardless of his wealth or who his father was, had one vote and one vote only.

Of course all of this was of no use whatsoever if you were a woman, a foreigner or a slave, but for everyone else it was phenomenal.

Cleisthenes also invented a way to stop people from screwing up the system, called **ostracism**. The name derived from *ostrakon:* pieces of broken pottery on which voters would write the names of anyone they felt the state could do without for a while. Every year the Ecclesia would take a vote on whether they felt the need for an ostracism; if so, and providing at least 6,000 votes were cast, the man whose name came up most often was exiled for ten years. By the time he came back, it was assumed, the issue about which he'd been kicking up a fuss would be old news, and he would have learned his lesson and would just sit at the back of the room and keep quiet from now on.

The Athenian Empire

Athens by this time had acquired quite an empire, which, along with territories loyal to Athens, extended north from the city and along the entire eastern coastline of modern-day Greece, across to Byzantium and down into the southwestern corner of

Turkey, encompassing almost all the islands of the Aegean. Growth in both population and wealth meant that the Athenians needed to import food and could export other things (they had discovered a nearby source of silver, and had plenty of slaves to mine it, which helped the balance of payments greatly). In short, they had become an international force to be reckoned with. And when that happens, history does tend to bring along someone who wants to reckon with you.

Enter the **Persians**. Skipping over that stuff about Nineveh and Cyaxares I mentioned earlier, what matters here is that for about a hundred years (*ca.* 550–465 B.C.), three Persian kings—**Cyrus** (known as "the Great"), **Darius** and **Xerxes**— steadily extended their sphere of influence across the eastern Mediterranean. They took over Lydia (the place in Asia Minor, not the character from *Pride and Prejudice*) and various Ionian Greek cities,* and inched their way into mainland Greece. The Greeks did not normally present a united front, but at a time like this they pulled together, in theory at least, against a common enemy.

Note the words *in theory*. The **Battle of Marathon** is a good example of how it worked in practice.

Date: 490 B.C. Scene: the plain of Marathon, about 23 miles (37 km) northeast of Athens. An Athenian force of 10,000 realizes

---

* *Ionian* or *Ionic* in this context refers to the area on the west coast of Asia Minor known as Ionia, which was part of the Athenian Empire until the Persians came along. It's not to be confused with the modern Ionian Sea, which lies to the west of Greece and contains Corfu and Kefalonia. Asia Minor is, for all intents and purposes, Turkey.

it is not strong enough to resist the invading Persians, so it sends its fastest runner, **Pheidippides**, to ask the Spartans for the help they had promised. The historian Herodotus (see page 62), never one to miss out on a good story, says that Pheidippides covered the distance—about 155 miles (250 km) each way—in two days. The Spartans, for reasons of their own, refused to set out before the full moon, by which time the Persians had somehow got confused about whether or not to attack Athens and had let the Athenians win after all. Pheidippides then ran from Marathon to Athens to announce the victory and dropped dead of exhaustion the moment the words were out of his mouth. (This last part may not be true—Herodotus says there is no evidence for it—but it certainly ought to be.[*])

This was under Darius, who died shortly afterward. The Persians did better when Darius's son Xerxes became king (see *Sparta*, page 65, for more about this). They even managed to sack Athens, but in 480 B.C. the Athenians bounced back under the leadership of a man named **Themistocles**. Thanks to him, Athens had built up a powerful navy, and he now came up with a cunning plan to lure the Persian fleet into a narrow channel separating the island of Salamis from the mainland. A resounding victory for the Athenians followed, and it was not long before the Persians were pushed out of Greece and the city-states could go back to fighting among themselves.

---

[*] The first "modern" marathons were run over distances varying from about 22 to 25 miles (35 to 40 km), roughly the distance from Athens to Marathon. Then, according to the website of the International Association of Athletics Federations, in 1908 the distance was officially set at 26 miles 385 yards (42.195 km).

About Greek historians

When you go back 1,500 years, it becomes a moot point where history ends and mythology begins. Few people would argue, however, that the greatest Greek historian was **Herodotus** (*ca.* 484–425 B.C.)—Cicero called him the father of history, and Cicero wasn't prone to admitting that anyone was better at anything than he was. Herodotus is said to have been the first to research and verify past events, which lifts him above his predecessors, known as *logographi* ("word writers"), who merely recorded oral traditions, without distinguishing between history and myth.

Most of Herodotus's writing deals with the Persian wars described in this chapter. Sometimes he excuses his many improbable anecdotes by saying, "I am obliged to record the things I am told, but I am certainly not required to believe them." On many occasions, he says firmly, "What I have here mentioned I saw with my own eyes." As I said in the Introduction, anyone who tells you the classics are dull hasn't read Herodotus.

Thucydides (*ca.* 460–400 B.C.): An Athenian who wrote an account of the Peloponnesian wars that some say is one of the greatest works of history ever. It's not an easy read, but it's remarkably unbiased and an astute analysis of the politics and strategy of the wars. Thucydides is also our source for Pericles's *Funeral Oration* (see page 64), though he thought Pericles was the bee's knees and may have spiced the speech up a little.

Xenophon (*ca.* 435–364 B.C.): A contemporary of Plato and pupil of Socrates. He never quite cut it as a philosopher, so he turned to soldiering and writing. His great work is the *Anabasis* ("expedition") *of Cyrus*, an account of the war between two Persian princes, Cyrus and Artaxerxes, when the latter had been chosen to succeed their father and the former was pissed off about it. (This is Cyrus the Younger, not to be confused with Cyrus the Great mentioned on page 60.) Xenophon was one of a force of 10,000 Greeks who supported Cyrus, so this is genuine eyewitness stuff—something that can't be said for all history.

Much later, **Plutarch** (*ca.* 46–120 A.D.) was not so much a historian as a biographer and moralist. Born in Greece, but spending part of his adult life in Rome, he wrote in Greek, as many "cultivated" Romans did at the time.* His *Parallel Lives* consists of twenty-three essays in which he compares a great Greek and a great Roman—Theseus, the legendary founder of Athens, and Romulus, ditto of Rome; the orators Demosthenes and Cicero; the generals Lysander and Sulla. Plutarch is interested in character rather than politics, so he chooses anecdotes "calculated to reveal the nature of the man"—which makes him great fun to read. He is also remarkably even-handed, neither groveling to the Romans (among whom he was living) nor being jingoistic about his fellow countrymen. Plutarch is the main source for Shakespeare's *Coriolanus, Julius Caesar* and *Antony and*

---

* He is said never to have mastered Latin, which surely adds to his charm for many of us.

Cleopatra, with lots of sumptuous details about Cleopatra's lifestyle: He describes a treasure consisting of "gold, silver, emeralds, pearls, ebony, ivory and cinnamon," which presumably means Cleopatra liked to look like Fanny Farmer when she was doing her baking.

Cue the beginning of the Golden Age

So, back to Athens, just in time to catch up with **Pericles**. Nothing to do with Shakespeare's *Prince of Tyre*, this Pericles held sway over what is known as the **Golden Age of Athens**, from the 450s B.C. until his death in 429 B.C.

Pericles was responsible for rebuilding the city after it was sacked by the Persians, and most notably commissioned the **Parthenon** (see page 124). He was a great orator, an important ability at a time when swathes of the electorate could neither read nor write, and was apparently incorruptible. He instigated reforms that took Athenian democracy to a new level: One was the introduction of state pay to members of the many juries scattered around the courts, ensuring that it was not only the rich who could afford to sit on them. At a time when Greeks were traveling, settling and intermarrying widely, Pericles also tightened up the definition of an Athenian citizen, encouraging Athenians to marry Athenians and preserve Athenian identity. As a committed enemy of Sparta, he was largely responsible for the outbreak of the **Peloponnesian Wars** (see page 66), which continued for twenty-five years after his death. His great *Funeral Oration*, given at a state funeral for the war dead, isn't really a eulogy at all but a celebration of

Athens and an exhortation to the Athenian people to live up to the standards of honor and courage demonstrated by the dead. Much of the decoration of the Parthenon is about just how honorable and brave the Athenians are, too. A man with a mission, you might say.

About Sparta

The word *spartan* has come into English to mean "restrained and unluxurious."* The Spartans prided themselves on their military prowess: From a very early age (some sources say as young as five), boys lived communally, were taught military discipline and toughened up by not being fed enough and none of this namby-pamby nonsense about asking for more, thank you very much. In the Spartans' own eyes at least, this was in stark contrast to the Athenians, whom they regarded as decadent, self-indulgent imperialists who did nothing but write great plays and produce great philosophers and rubbish like that. The Spartans believed in oligarchy—rule by the few. The needs of the individual were subservient to those of the state, and for a long time this was a genuine ideological difference between the two cities.

The ruling Spartan military class was vastly outnumbered by its one-up-from-the-slaves population, the Helots, a subjugated people from another part of the Peloponnese

---

* Sparta was in the region of Laconia, from which we derive another useful word, *laconic*, meaning never uttering more words than are strictly necessary—a further example of the Spartans' spartan approach to life.

(that bit stuck on the bottom of Greece, joined to the rest of the country by the Isthmus of Corinth). Because the Helots were all of the same race and spoke the same language—which was not the case in Athens, nor later in Rome, where laboring populations came from all over the place—there was always a risk that they would unite to overthrow their masters. This is part of the reason why Sparta never became a great imperial power: The Spartans needed to be on constant military alert, turning themselves into what the world expert on the subject, Professor Paul Cartledge, calls Fortress Sparta, because the risks from within were every bit as great as those from outside.

Sparta was important for about 120 years, between 480 and 360 B.C. At the start of this period it led the Greek defense against Persian invasion, making a name for itself at the **Battle of Thermopylae** (480 B.C.), where a ridiculously small army comprising 300 Spartan champions under **King Leonidas** resisted the massive Persian forces for two days.* Although technically a defeat, this heroic stand had a hugely morale-boosting effect on the Greeks and inspired continued resistance.

The Persians thoroughly dealt with, intercity warfare picked up again. From about 461 to 446 B.C., and then again for almost thirty years from 431 B.C., Athens and Sparta fought what are known as the **Peloponnesian Wars**.

---

* These were hard men: They thought the Persians were wimps for using arrows in order to avoid hand-to-hand combat.

Sparta emerged victorious thanks, ironically enough, to the support of a Persian fleet.

The defeat of Athens left the way clear for Sparta to attack a few neighbors, but seizing the citadel in Thebes proved a deeply unpopular move. Thebes defeated Sparta at the **Battle of Leuctra** in 371 B.C. and Sparta was pretty much never heard of again. Athens and Thebes then squabbled their way through a few more decades until Philip of Macedon came along and banged their heads together (see page 68).

Apart from Leonidas, practically the only famous person to have come out of Sparta is its naval commander **Lysander**, who crops up in the old patriotic song "The British Grenadiers": "Some talk of Alexander and some of Hercules/ Of Hector and Lysander and such great names as these," and so on. And even he is probably only really famous if you have ever belonged to the British Grenadiers. The young lover in Shakespeare's *A Midsummer Night's Dream* came from Athens and has nothing to do with any of this.

Off with the old…

After being defeated by Sparta, Athens ceased to be an important power, although some of the playwrights were still going strong and the philosophers had hardly started (see Chapters 6 and 9), so we shouldn't write it off altogether. But its fall coincided with the rise of **Macedon** and left the way clear for the conquering achievements of **Alexander the Great** (see overleaf).

One more name before we finish with Athens, though: The orator **Demosthenes** came to the fore at this time, because he was an ardent opponent of any form of appeasement of Macedon. His passionate eloquence persuaded the Athenians to hold out against the proposed **Hellenic confederacy** (that's the formal name for Philip of Macedon's plan for world domination, which we'll come to in a minute) for a while, but more important for our purposes his speeches continued to be studied and rote-learned by anyone interested in public speaking for the next thousand years. He is generally regarded as the greatest orator of all time, no mean feat for someone who started life with a speech impediment and cured it by speaking with stones in his mouth until his diction improved.

Alexander the Great

Reflecting on how little many of us accomplish in life, Tom Lehrer (political satirist) once said that "when Mozart was my age, he had been dead for two years."

If that idea upsets you, don't read this section.

Alexander (ruled 336–323 B.C.) was the son of Philip II of Macedon, who had in the course of his reign subdued the barbarian tribes to the north of his kingdom and imposed his will on the warring Greek city-states to the south by creating the

League of Corinth, of which he proclaimed himself head, and forcing the Greeks to join it. Perhaps unsurprisingly, Philip was assassinated and Alexander became king at the age of twenty.

Macedon or Macedonia comprised the province of northern Greece that stills bears its name, plus what is now the former Yugoslav republic, plus part of modern Bulgaria. Most of the land to the east was ruled by the Persians. So, after quickly checking that the Greeks were under control and could be trusted to behave themselves while he was away, Alexander set off to conquer the rest of the known world.* Some authorities say that his intention was to create a cosmopolitan blend of European and Asian cultures and a multiracial society (he married at least two Asian women and forced his officers to do the same); others suggest this was just an excuse to extend his dominions, besiege or massacre anything or anyone that stood in his way. It could have been a bit of both.

Certainly he was a great general, combining the prudence to consolidate his position and establish adequate garrisons before moving on, with the ability to make quick and ingenious decisions that took the enemy by surprise. He is often compared to Napoleon, and not just because both were vertically challenged egomaniacs.

Having sorted out Asia Minor, Alexander marched south along the east coast of the Mediterranean, successfully besieged Tyre and Gaza and, his reputation going before him, strolled pretty

---

* The term *known world* is a decidedly Eurocentric one in this context. What the Chinese or the Mayans knew at this time is beyond the scope of this book.

much unopposed into Egypt. Turning east, he went through five years of guerrilla warfare in modern-day Iraq and Iran. He eventually destroyed the ancient Persian capital, Persepolis, and, by crossing the River Indus (in modern Pakistan), extended his realm beyond anything that the Persians had conquered.

By this time his men were exhausted and close to mutiny, so Alexander turned back to Babylon, which he had decided to make his capital. He died there of a sudden fever a year later, a month short of his thirty-third birthday.

Alexander's empire fell apart pretty quickly after his death, but he left one lasting legacy—a **Hellenic** or "Grecianized" world (*Hellas* being the Greek name for Greece). Thanks largely to Alexander, the area from the middle of the Mediterranean to the north of modern India, including almost all of what we now call the Middle East and northern Egypt, spoke a common language and shared cultural ideas. The Hellenic period was as rich in the development of arts and science as the Athenian Golden Age: **Archimedes**, **Epicurus** and **Zeno**, founder of Stoicism, all came along at this time (more about them in Chapters 8 and 9), and **Alexandria**, with its huge library,* became the great center for scholarship.

All this lasted for a couple of hundred years until some other conquering power came along and decided that everyone should speak Latin. Now who could that have been?

---

* At its peak it is said to have housed 700,000 volumes, a figure that the Bodleian Library in Oxford didn't match until the early twentieth century.

5

The Old Stuff II: Roman History

We'll see when we get to the chapter on literature that the ancestor of the Romans was a Trojan prince called **Aeneas**. Which will confuse you if you think that Rome was founded by **Romulus** and **Remus**. It's another of those areas where mythology flows into history and you just have to go with it.

Romulus and Remus

The story that links the descendants of Aeneas with Romulus and Remus is a complicated one, but here it is in a nutshell: Numitor, the king of an ancient Italian city called Alba Longa, had a daughter named Rhea Silvia. She became pregnant by the god Mars (don't ask) and produced twin sons, who were thrown into the River Tiber by Numitor's rival. Miraculously washed ashore, the babies were found and suckled by a she-wolf, brought up by a shepherd and eventually recognized by whoever needed to recognize them. At a key moment some birds flew overhead, suggesting that the lads should build a new city and that Romulus should be king of it. Remus was understandably put out by this arbitrary bit of favoritism. In a fit of petulance, and with a deplorable lack of tact considering his brother was about to become king of the most important city in the world, he marched up to the foundations, said "That's not much of a wall"—which it wasn't; the builders had only just started, having been held up on another job—and jumped over. Romulus killed him and carried on building.

In order to provide wives for his followers, Romulus carried off a number of women from a neighboring tribe (famous painting by Poussin, *The Rape of the Sabines*, in the Louvre) and settled down to be the first king of Rome.

The traditional date for the founding of the city is 753 B.C., and Roman dates were calculated based on this: A.U.C. or *ab urbe condita*, "from the founding of the city."

The seven hills of Rome

Pub quiz time. Everyone knows that Rome is built on seven hills. (So is Cincinnati, but for some reason not as much fuss is made about that.) They are the **Palatine**, the **Quirinal**, the **Viminal**, the **Capitoline** (which today encompasses much of central Rome), the **Caelian**, the **Esquiline** and the **Aventine**. Although Romulus's settlement began on the Palatine, the **Capitol** or citadel on the summit of the Capitoline was the site of the most important temple of early times, the Temple of Jupiter Optimus Maximus (that's "the best *and* the greatest," so don't mess with him) and of Juno and Minerva. In 390 B.C., the Gauls invaded Rome in the dead of night. As they were sneaking up the hill, Juno's sacred geese (they lived in the temple) put up such a cacking fuss that they woke the guards. The Capitol was successfully defended, and the geese continued to be sacred (and fed at great public expense) for centuries afterward.

The Capitol was also the location of the **Tarpeian Rock**, from which condemned traitors were hurled to their deaths.

In the early years of the empire, the Palatine was the upscale area—if you climb the hill behind the **Forum,** you can see the ruins of palaces belonging to Augustus and his wife Livia. But that is getting ahead of ourselves. Long before that there was ...

The Roman Kingdom

After Romulus came six more kings:

• Numa Pompilius
• Tullius Hostilius
• Ancus Marcius
• Tarquinius Priscus
• Servius Tullius
• Tarquinius Superbus

Superbus doesn't mean "superb" in this context, it means "proud and tyrannical," and Tarquin was, very; so in 510 B.C. the Romans threw him out and founded a republic. If you are old enough to have read Macaulay's *Lays of Ancient Rome*, you may remember that this is the time when Horatius and two companions "kept the bridge" by holding off the forces of Lars Porsena of Clusium, who was supporting Tarquin, to give the Romans time to chop the bridge down behind them and prevent the enemy from crossing the Tiber and entering Rome. Horatius sent the other two scampering back across the bridge just before it collapsed, then dived into the river and swam back—to mighty cheers from one side and great gnashing of teeth from the other.

About Gaul

Why bother with a bit about Gaul? It's just France, right? Not quite, but don't worry, I won't keep you long.

In the really old days, much of northern Italy was occupied by Celtic tribes known as **Gauls**, and the area was called **Cisalpine Gaul** (meaning it was on this side of the Alps, as far as the Romans were concerned). It was from here that the Gauls raided Rome off and on, including the time they were rumbled by the geese (see page 73), until the Romans finally got fed up and took over the entire area in the first century B.C.

On the other side of the Alps was **Transalpine Gaul** (easy enough, isn't it, once you get the hang of it?). This was one of the first areas the Romans conquered. They called it "our province" or simply "Provincia," a name that lives on as modern Provence.

By the time Caesar wrote that "all of Gaul was divided into three parts," however, he was more or less talking about modern France, with a bit of Belgium, the Netherlands and so forth thrown it. Defining the three parts, he explained that the River Garonne separated the Aquitani from the Gauls, who occupied the area up to about Paris and east into Switzerland; beyond that were the Belgae.* Between 58 and 51 B.C., Caesar conquered all of it. The last general to resist him was Vercingetorix, who won a great victory at Gergovia, not far from Clermont-Ferrand, but succumbed shortly afterward.

The Roman Republic

The Roman Republic† was essentially an aristocracy, in the original sense of the word, which means that it was ruled by the aristocrats—formally known as **patricians**. The rest of the Roman citizens were known as **plebeians**, meaning "of the common people."

The main governing body was the **Senate**, at first made up of 300 patricians (they let plebeians in later) who were in charge of advising the **magistrates** on almost all aspects of civil and military government. The word *advising* is something of a

---

* There is no record that Caesar ever said "If it's Tuesday it must be Helvetia," but it would have been in keeping with this slightly broad-brushstroke attitude to geography.

† The word comes from the Latin *res publica*, meaning "a public matter."

euphemism here, because in reality there had to be a very good reason for a magistrate to go against the will of the Senate.

Sorting out the system didn't happen overnight, but by and large the magistrates were elected by popular vote (of the male citizens, of course) and served for a year at a time. The most important of them were the two **consuls**, who acted as judges, oversaw the civil service and commanded the army (the word for the right to command the army was *imperium*, hence *imperial*, *emperor* and *empire*, of which more later). The two consuls had to agree about any decision and each had the power of *veto* ("I forbid" in Latin) over the other. Their bodyguards, called **lictors**, carried bundles of rods, sometimes containing an axe; these were called **fasces** (which simply meant "bundles," but from which ultimately the word *fascism* derives).

Below the consuls came two **praetors**, who were in charge of civil law but were also entitled to command an army[*]; then a number of **aediles**, who ran all sorts of domestic matters from organizing games to mending the sewers; and **quaestors**, who looked after various bits of public expenditure.

In addition to this group, there were two **censors**, elected for an eighteen-month term every five years, ostensibly to conduct a census and carry out ritual purification. In fact they seem to have spent most of their time punishing people—even

---

[*] Hence the Praetorian Guard, who by imperial times were basically the emperor's bodyguard and an immensely powerful bunch. Tradition has it that it was the guards who placed Claudius on the throne when Caligula was assassinated (see page 93) and the Senate was dithering about what to do.

to the extent of removing someone from the Senate or stripping a man of his Roman citizenship.

And there were two plebeian **assemblies**, one military and one civilian, and two plebeian **tribunes**, who represented the interests of the people and were the only officials to have the power of veto over the Senate.

This basic system held sway for more than 400 years, with the balance of power between Senate, consuls and tribunes teetering back and forth depending on the personalities of the individuals concerned, the economic needs of the moment and whether there was any major fighting to be done. As time went by, the rich-poor divide increased, with powerful plebeians tending to lose touch with the concerns of the less-powerful plebeians, who should have been their primary fan base. Two important names at this point are the **Gracchus** (plural **Gracchi**) **brothers**, Tiberius and Gaius, powerful tribunes of the second century B.C. They instituted reforms to extend land ownership among the poor, which brought them into conflict with the powers that be: Both came to unpleasant ends, but they are celebrated by some as the founders of socialism.

As Rome increased its influence abroad, military campaigns might be fought simultaneously in more than one outpost, so more than one general could be rising to prominence (and wealth and power) while another person was running the show at home.

It's asking for trouble, isn't it? Read on…

About Carthage

Carthage had become such a thorn in the flesh of the Romans by the second century B.C. that the great censor Cato the Elder was going around saying *delenda est Carthago*— "Carthage must be destroyed." So what was that all about?

Carthage was situated on the coast of North Africa, in modern Tunisia (you can visit the remains while you're lapping up some cheap winter sun). It was founded by a people the Greeks called **Phoenicians**, and in mythological times it was ruled over by **Dido**, the queen who features in Virgil's *Aeneid* (see page 113). The name *Phoenician* derives from the Greek for purple or crimson, because the Phoenicians were particularly skilled in dyeing cloth this color. They had another claim to fame, too: The Greek alphabet is based on the Phoenician one, so the Phoenicians were probably the first people to use letters as opposed to pictograms for writing.[*]

By the middle of the third century B.C., Carthage had risen to be a considerable power, the only one in the west that rivaled Rome. Although the Roman Empire *per se* was still over two centuries away, the Romans never missed a chance to annex anywhere that would provide grain, manpower or tax revenue, and a twenty-three-year spat known as the **First Punic War**[†] resulted in the Romans taking control of Sicily.

---

[*] One claim to fame the Phoenicians seem to lack is the invention of the fantastical bird that is reborn from its own ashes. The concept of the phoenix seems to have originated in India, and didn't reach Greece until the first or second century A.D. The Greeks presumably decided that purple was the only color for such a groovy bird and named it accordingly.

[†] The Latin for *Phoenician* is *Punicus*, hence the name.

But the Carthaginians were not crushed by this war, and within thirty years they were back, this time with a great general called **Hannibal** (247–182 B.C.). Hannibal marched through Spain (which was part of the Carthaginian empire), crossed the Alps into Italy and headed for Rome. He'd won a succession of battles in order to get this far, and once he reached Italy he had a great victory at Cannae, but not much after that; he was eventually forced to retreat back to Africa, where he was defeated once and for all at the Battle of Zama in 202 B.C.

Carthage continued to be important, though, at least in Africa, and soon came into conflict with Rome again. The Romans' stated goal in the **Third Punic War** (Hannibal's having been the second) was to destroy Carthage completely, which they did after a siege in 146 B.C.

The city was later restored and it thrived again until the Arabs destroyed it in the seventh century A.D., but 146 B.C. marked the end of it as a world power. Today there are five cities in the United States named Carthage, though, and one named Hannibal, so the memory lingers on.

But, I can hear you saying, "Who cares? What about the elephants?" Well, yes, Hannibal did have elephants. It's one of those urban myths that is actually true. Livy (see page 99) mentions that there were forty of them. In one battle they "terrified the horses not only by their appearance but by their unaccustomed smell, and caused widespread panic."

Marius and Sulla

Marius did well in wars against a North African king called Jugurtha and was elected consul in 107 B.C. His plebeian background led him to support the power of the tribunes, which meant weakening the Senate and the consuls. Despite the fact that his party was allegedly the democratic, "popular" one, he broke a lot of the rules and put his own cronies into office without the formality of elections.

All this brought him into conflict with an aristocrat called **Sulla**, who was busy out east fighting a king named Mithridates, a potentially prestigious gig that Marius had wanted for himself. In 86 B.C., Sulla marched on Rome, forcing Marius to flee to Africa. Sulla then headed back east, but a year or two later, having made peace with Mithridates, he marched his army to Rome, took control of the city and proclaimed himself dictator. Which wasn't exactly in the rule book either.

Marius was dead by this time, but there were enough of his party left to turn the next couple of years into a pretty bloody civil war, from which Sulla emerged triumphant. He introduced massive constitutional reforms, restoring the power of the Senate at the expense of the tribunes. He also popularized a handy way of dealing with opponents, known as **proscription**: He simply stuck their names up on a post in the Forum and decreed that they no longer had any human rights—*ergo* (that's Latin for "therefore" and it seems not too show-offy to throw it in here), it was perfectly OK for anyone to murder them. And believe me, they did. In droves.

Rather surprisingly Sulla died in his bed in 78 B.C.. He merited the first-ever state funeral for a Roman citizen—which puts him on a par with U.S. presidents and Winston Churchill, in that respect if in no other. But he had paved the way for a protégé who took Rome pretty promptly into another civil war.

About Latin names

The Greeks kept names simple, tending to have only one, and to append "son of X" if they needed to distinguish one Aristophanes or one Zeno from another, though when democracy caught on (see page 56), they began to add the name of their deme instead.

The Romans were more orderly about it, and most of them—or at least most patricians—had three names, called respectively the **praenomen, nomen** and **cognomen.**

The **praenomen** (forename) was the personal name—what your mother called you—and there were surprisingly few of these: Marcus, Gaius, Publius; names like Quintus and Sextus (fifth and sixth), which showed that your parents already had lots of sons and were running out of ideas, and not a lot else. No Samuels, Archies or Kevins.

The **nomen** (name) was the name of the clan or gens, effectively an extended family. It always ended in -*ius;* famous ones included Julius and Claudius, a combination of which produced the Julio-Claudian dynasty that was responsible for the first handful of emperors (see page 89).

The **cognomen** (additional name) was initially a nickname but came to be transferred from father to son, so that it became more like a modern surname. It almost always denoted a physical characteristic, but because it stuck to a family through generations, it was not always relevant to the individual who bore it: *Caesar*, for example, probably means "hairy," and we know that Julius Caesar went bald and took great pains to disguise it.

A fourth name, the **agnomen** (another additional nickname), was sometimes added to mark a personal achievement or to signify adoption, so you end up with mouthfuls such as Gaius Julius Caesar Octavianus, which meant Gaius, originally of the Octavian clan, adopted by Julius Caesar (he changed his name to the Emperor Augustus, and who can blame him?). The Emperor Claudius's father was dubbed Germanicus, because he had been victorious in battles against various German tribes; Claudius, his elder brother and his nephew, who became Caligula, all adopted that name to add to the plenty that they already had.

Women at first had only one name, the feminine form of their father's nomen. So Catullus's Lesbia (see page 110) was only ever called Clodia, Octavian's sister who married Mark Antony was Octavia, and so on. Later women also used another name belonging to their husband or one or other parent, but—rather outrageously—there were no female praenomens.

Pompey and Caesar

Pompey* had been a supporter of Sulla and had fought successful campaigns against the Marius faction in Spain, Sicily and Africa. Having served as consul, he was put in charge of the armies in the eastern Mediterranean, where he was immensely successful, but on his return to Rome ran up against that rising young star **Julius Caesar**.

Caesar had had an exciting early life, including being captured by pirates while on the run from Sulla's wrath, but by the time we are talking about—62 B.C.—he was firmly on the political ladder. It was about this time that he divorced his second (or third, depending on whom you read) wife, **Pompeia**. *The Cambridge Biographical Dictionary* says this was because of "a fertility rite scandal in which she had been involved." That's a tantalizing piece of information, isn't it? What happened was that Roman ladies held a festival in honor of the Good Goddess, an otherwise unnamed deity who looked after women. Men were not allowed to attend, but in the course of the celebration, Pompeia had an assignation with **Clodius** (see page 110), who defiled the proceedings just by being there, never mind anything he may or may not have done with Pompeia.

Although Clodius was tried for impiety, Caesar refused to testify against him (perhaps for political reasons, to keep in with the mass of the Roman people, who were very pro Clodius) and

---

* His proper name was Gnaeus Pompeius, and through his various successes in battle he had earned the nickname Magnus—"the Great"—while still in his twenties. Interesting that no one thought *he* was getting above himself and needed to be assassinated.

he got off. When asked why he had nevertheless dismissed his wife, Caesar replied, "I wished my wife to be not so much as suspected." Hence the expression "Caesar's wife must be above suspicion," which has survived long after (the probably very suspect) Pompeia has been forgotten. Subsequent to this Caesar married **Calpurnia** who, according to Shakespeare, had a dream foreseeing his murder and begged him not to go to the Senate that day. Above suspicion she may have been, but she'd have ruined a brilliant play if anyone had listened to her.

Enough of this domestic gossip. The important thing is that Caesar wasn't prepared to kowtow to Pompey, nor Pompey to him. Additionally, there was an immensely wealthy man called **Crassus** who couldn't be ignored—and he and Pompey loathed each other. An awkward situation when all three of them had armies at their backs.

There are a number of good stories about Crassus, one of which is mentioned in the footnote on page 141. He was also the general who finally overcame **Spartacus**, an escaped gladiator who put together a vast army of slaves and runaways, and defeated the Roman army on a number of occasions between 73 and 71 B.C. If you are of the generation that thinks of Spartacus as Kirk Douglas, then Crassus was Laurence Olivier.*

---

* Spartacus himself was killed in battle, not crucified, but apart from that minor detail the last scene in Kubrick's film, with 6,000 of Spartacus's followers nailed up along the Appian Way, has its basis in history. At least, that is what we are told by a later historian named—in one of those happy coincidences that make the study of trivia so rewarding—Appian.

Anyway, Caesar, realizing that trouble was brewing, suggested the three of them divide control of the Roman provinces between them. This was, it has to be said, bypassing the "let's elect someone democratically for a year" principle that was still theoretically in place.

This arrangement—often called the **First Triumvirate**—fell apart when Crassus died in 53 B.C. (The historian Dio Cassius later tells the story that the Parthians defeated Crassus in battle and forced him to drink molten gold as an ironic punishment for his thirst for riches.) By this time Caesar had conquered much of Gaul (see page 74) and tried invading Britain. As his power grew over the next few years, the Senate in Rome became more and more anxious and eventually ordered him to return to Rome without his army. Caesar obeyed only the first part of this command and by crossing the River Rubicon—which marked the boundary between Cisalpine Gaul and the Roman Republic—at the head of an army, committed an act of treason. The Roman forces sent to stop him were commanded by—any guesses?—Pompey.

Battles between them meandered all over the empire (we might as well start calling it that—the republic is on its last legs by now and the first emperor will be making his entrance, admittedly under an assumed name, in a couple of paragraphs' time) until Pompey was finally defeated at the **Battle of Pharsalus** in 48 B.C.; he sought refuge in Egypt and was murdered there on the orders of the Egyptian prince **Ptolemy**, seeking to curry favor with Caesar. Caesar, disgusted by this breach of trust, put Ptolemy's sister **Cleopatra** on the Egyptian throne instead. Pausing only to have an affair with her (see the play by George Bernard Shaw, in which she smuggles herself into his presence rolled in a carpet), Caesar went off to win a quick battle in Asia Minor—after which he declared, *Veni, vidi, vici* (I came, I saw, I conquered)—and a few more in other outposts of the empire. He then returned to Rome to be assassinated.

According to Shakespeare, the motives of Caesar's assassins were entirely honorable. In *Julius Caesar* he shows the conspirators **Brutus** and **Cassius** fearing that Caesar was about to be proclaimed king, which they thought would destroy the liberties that Roman citizens enjoyed under the republic. And speaking of Shakespeare, opinions vary as to whether Caesar actually said, *"Et tu, Brute?"* as he died. There are no reliable eyewitness reports and—as ever— lots of people making up their own versions.

One other thing before we leave Caesar: He found time to reform the **calendar**. Before this, a normal year had been 355 days long, with what are called intercalary months inserted every now and then to bring the calendar into line with the solar year. Caesar's advisers worked out that 365¼ days was nearer the mark, so in 45 B.C. he decreed that most years would be 365 days long and instituted the leap year, which gave an extra day every four years, as it does to this day.

The Roman calendar had had twelve months for a long time, but the year had started around the spring equinox (traditionally, though not accurately, March 25). Caesar decided that the year should start nearer the winter solstice, so January became the first month. Which explains why September, October, November and December—whose names mean the seventh, eighth, ninth and tenth months— became the ninth, tenth, eleventh and twelfth. There also used to be months called Quintilis and Sextilis—the fifth and sixth—but these were renamed in honor of Julius Caesar and his successor, Augustus. By the way, the really imaginative guy who couldn't think of any better names for the months than Fifth, Sixth and so on was Romulus, who must have run out of energy after he had built a city and wrought havoc on the Sabine people.

We now know that Caesar's system wasn't perfect either, but the **Julian Calendar**, as it was called, hung in there until Pope Gregory XIII changed it in 1582. So it couldn't have been all that bad.

About the Roman calendar

The Romans calculated dates by working backward. Each month had three key dates, the **Calends** (hence the word *calendar*), the **Nones** and the **Ides**. The Calends was always on the first of the month, the Nones and Ides usually on the fifth and thirteenth, except in March, May, July and

---

October, when they fell on the seventh and the fifteenth (like so much else in life, it was to do with the phases of the moon). So a date was given as "three days before the Ides" or "ten days before the Calends." And, just to make it more complicated, they counted the days at both ends, so where we would say that March 12 was three days before the Ides (the fifteenth), they would have said it was four.

The Greeks didn't work their dates in this way, so the old-fashioned idiom "the Greek calends" meant never, because there was no such day.[*]

An interesting footnote to this, courtesy of a wonderful book called *The Calendar* by David Ewing Duncan: This system was still in use a thousand years after the collapse of the Roman Empire. When Shakespeare had a soothsayer warn Julius Caesar to beware the Ides of March, he could safely assume that his 1590s audience would know what he meant.

And after Caesar?

Public opinion quickly turned against the assassins, so Brutus and Cassius fled from Rome. This left **Mark Antony**, Caesar's friend and supporter who had officially shared consulship

---

[*] The Greek calendar was so complicated that everyone who ever knew anything about it has wiped it out of their memory banks. The Athenians had a civil year and a Bouleutic year, the latter concerned with when the Boule or Senate held office. The two years were calculated in different ways, had different numbers of days, and involved solstices and new moons and intercalary months and goodness knows what else. Plus they applied only in Athens. Practically every city-state had its own system.

with him at the time of the assassination, in charge. However, Caesar had an adopted son and heir, **Octavian**, who was not about to be passed over in the rush for power. He raised an army, defeated Antony and got himself proclaimed consul, but, on Antony's return with another army, backed down and agreed to form a triumvirate.* Antony meanwhile defeated Brutus and Cassius at the **Battle of Philippi** (powerful stuff in Shakespeare's version), and then took time out with Cleopatra in Egypt (Shakespeare covered this, too, in a separate play).

The next ten years were full of quarrels and complications, including Antony marrying Octavian's sister **Octavia** in an attempt to heal the rift, but in the end Octavian managed to turn public opinion against Antony; Antony and Cleopatra were defeated at the **Battle of Actium** (31 B.C.) and both committed suicide, leaving Octavian free to change his name to **Augustus** and get on with the business of being emperor. Augustus later boasted that he found Rome brick and left it marble, but my guess is that it was marble all the time—you just couldn't tell because it was covered in blood.

The Roman Empire

The Roman Empire was a masterpiece of administration, probably the greatest of its kind there has ever been. At its

---

* Because they'd always worked out so well in the past, of course… The third member of this triumvirate was a nonentity called Lepidus, who was basically there to make up the numbers.

fullest extent, it stretched from Scotland to North Africa, from Spain across to eastern Turkey and Armenia, down through Israel and over into Iraq. It was ruled by the same legal system, and its sixty million people all officially used the same language (they didn't all speak it as their mother tongue, but Latin was the language of administration). In a time when it took a minimum of three days to sail from the Roman port of Ostia to Marseille, on the nearest coast of the nearest province, and when if you wanted to travel anywhere by road you probably had to build it first, this was staggering.

And yet it was run by some of the maddest, baddest and most dangerous men ever to have graced the history books. Here's a rundown of some of the most significant of them. The first few were all related and belonged to what was called the **Julio-Claudian line**. A lot of intermarrying went on, which may help to explain why each generation seems to have been more bonkers than the one before.

Augustus (ruled 27 B.C.–A.D. 14): Once things settled down and people accepted the idea of an emperor, Augustus presided over a time of immense prosperity and a damn sight more peace than the Romans had seen for a century. He was a consummate politician and, strangely for a man in his position, had a great respect for the forms of government and for the concept of a budget. Or if he didn't he could certainly talk the talk. He also presided over a Golden Age of literature and the arts (see page 110). The Augustan Age was so, well, august that the term was applied centuries later to the high spot of French drama, and to

English literature in the early eighteenth century, when people such as Alexander Pope were imitating Virgil and Horace. But Augustus's reign was also a time of—how shall I put this?—a certain laxity of morals. The emperor himself was rather austere, approved of marriage and old-fashioned family values, and didn't eat or drink too much, but he was fighting a losing battle where that was concerned. See page 114 for a bit of tabloid gossip about his daughter, for instance.

About Roman citizens and slaves

Unlike the Athenians, the Romans conferred **citizenship** on a lot of the peoples they conquered. Citizenship gave a man the right to vote, to make contracts and to enter into a legal marriage. It also gave him the obligation to pay taxes and to do military service: One of the arguments for making a "barbarian" a citizen was that he could then be co-opted into the army. Women weren't allowed to vote or run for public office, but they had more freedom than in a lot of Western cultures over the ensuing millennia: They could own property and become rich in their own right, and the Roman matron was a respected figure in society.

The poorest Roman citizen might own a slave or two, and rich households had many. Slaves—who were mostly prisoners of war or the victims of pirates' raids—could be freed by their masters, a process called **manumission**, as a reward for loyal service. They could also save up any

---

money that came their way—tips and bribes, presumably—
and eventually buy their freedom.

The **freedman** of a Roman citizen was not allowed to hold
public office, but many held positions of trust within the
home of their previous master or became influential "special
advisers": The Emperor Claudius, perhaps not the sharpest
knife in the box, was widely criticized for allowing a
number of freedmen, nominally his secretaries, to have too
much power.[*]

Even so, there was no shortage of slaves in Rome. The
figures are vague, but in the time of Augustus the population
of the city was probably a bit over a million, and slaves
almost certainly made up at least 25 percent and possibly
as much as 50 percent of the total number. No citizen was
really worried about having to iron his own toga.

Tiberius (A.D. 14–37): The son of Augustus's wife Livia, but
not of Augustus; she assured her son's succession by
systematically murdering or arranging the disgrace of
everyone who might stand in his way, including, rumor has
it, Augustus himself. Some say that Augustus suspected she
was trying to poison him and refused to eat anything except
figs that he had picked himself. Livia, rising to the occasion,
painted poison on to the figs while they were still on the tree.

---

[*] One of them, Narcissus, was responsible for the summary execution of
Claudius's rampantly unfaithful wife Messalina and one of her lovers, so there
may be an element of truth in this.

Anyway, Tiberius became emperor. He was in his fifties by then, with a strong track record in administration and military matters, but he had none of Augustus's flair. His supporters say that he was deeply unhappy because he had been forced, for political reasons, to divorce the woman he loved and marry Augustus's promiscuous daughter Julia. His detractors say he retired to Capri to indulge his loathsome sexual depravities. They may all be right. Anyway, members of the royal family kept dropping like flies—Livia wasn't the only one who went in for poisoning—so that by the time Tiberius died, the most obvious candidate for the throne was his twenty-five-year-old great-nephew...

Gaius Caligula (37–41): A distinguished pedigree—great-grandson of both Augustus and Mark Antony—but crazy despite all that. *Caligula* means "little boot," a nickname he earned as a child because he was brought up in an army camp and wore little boots. He is said to have thought he was a god or the Jews' much-discussed Messiah, to have made his horse a consul,* slept with and impregnated at least one of his sisters, and generally shed blood and wasted money with extraordinary abandon. He came, unsurprisingly, to an unpleasant end.

Claudius (41–54): The "I, Claudius" of the novel and TV series; Caligula's uncle, chosen by the Praetorian Guard (see footnote, page 76) to replace him before the blood was dry on

---

* That happened a lot. It allowed the miscreant (normally an aristocrat) to do the decent thing and, more important, not forfeit his property to the state and leave his family destitute, which is what would have happened if he had been tried and condemned.

the assassins' swords. Suetonius describes Claudius as "so weak in understanding as to be the common sport of the emperor's household"; certainly he was more a scholar than a politician. Nonetheless, he was the emperor who finally made Britain a Roman province, traveling there himself. He entered into a number of disastrous marriages; his fourth wife Agrippina was the mother of…

Nero (54–68): There is no evidence that he fiddled while Rome burned, nor that he started the fire himself, though, as the saying goes, "The rumors persist." *The Cambridge Biographical Encyclopedia* sums him up beautifully: "Nero, more interested in sex, singing, acting and chariot-racing than government, neglected affairs of state [I should think he did—where would he have found the time?] and corruption set in." He was overthrown by the army and forced to commit suicide,* but not before he had found time to have his own mother murdered.

There were no relatives left to succeed him, so, on the one hand, good riddance; on the other, oh dear, there's a vacancy. You might think that anything that happened after Nero would have been an improvement, but you had to get through 69 A.D.—the year of the four emperors—before that turned out to be true. **Galba**, **Otho** and **Vitellius** came and went within a matter of months and were followed by:

---

* That happened a lot. It allowed the miscreant (normally an aristocrat) to do the decent thing and, more important, not forfeit his property to the state and leave his family destitute, which is what would have happened if he had been tried and condemned.

Vespasian (69–79): A successful general, proclaimed emperor by his troops as a way of putting an end to the civil wars of the previous year. One of the few emperors with a modicum of common sense, he presided over a decade of relative calm and started the building of the Colosseum (see page 137). On his deathbed he is alleged to have said, "My goodness, I think I am turning into a god!" So some of the loony Julio-Claudian blood must have rubbed off on him by the end.

Titus (79–81): Vespasian's elder son. During his father's reign he managed to offend the Jews for all eternity by destroying Jerusalem; as emperor he was in charge at the time of the eruption of Vesuvius that buried Pompeii and Herculaneum. Let's be charitable and say that the second part of this wasn't his fault.

Domitian (81–96): Younger brother of Titus. There was a lot of great architecture going on at this time, and Domitian built an immense palace on the Palatine Hill and an arch in memory of his brother. The latter is still more or less intact and is one of the highlights of the Forum (see page 129). However, he turned into a complete tyrant, behaved as if he were a god (yes, another one) and was assassinated. End of another dynasty.

Nerva (96–98): A senator promoted because he was considered a safe pair of hands. He was the first of what the Italian Renaissance writer and politician Machiavelli later called "the five good emperors." They had, Machiavelli said, "no need of praetorian cohorts, or of countless legions to guard them, but were defended by their own good lives, the goodwill of their subjects, and the attachment of the senate." Maybe, but Nerva, well-meaning though he was, didn't win the goodwill of his subjects, and the Praetorian Guard made him adopt Trajan so that they knew they would be happy with what they were getting next.*

Trajan (98–117): Rome still boasts the remnants of Trajan's column, Trajan's baths, Trajan's forum—he was a busy man. A great soldier, he extended the Roman Empire (whose borders hadn't changed much for a hundred years) to its greatest ever area, going as far east as the Persian Gulf. Also, fascinatingly, he had a Beatles haircut, some 1,860 years before Brian Epstein invented it all over again.

Hadrian (117–138): Ah, now, we know about him. The man with the wall, indeed a number of walls. He believed in defending the existing empire rather than trying to extend it. The amazing thing about Hadrian is the way he managed to stay in power while spending almost no time in Rome, and this becomes all the more amazing when you consider that the Roman Senate hated him. At the very beginning of his reign, when Hadrian himself was out east, four senior senators were executed in suspect circumstances, possibly because they had been plotting against the new emperor, and the relationship between emperor and Senate never healed. So Hadrian just

---

* Adopting someone as your chosen successor happened a lot, too. None of the five "good" emperors was the son of his predecessor.

stayed away. He traveled to Britain, he traveled to Greece, he traveled to Africa, he inspected troops and garrisons and reformed anything he thought was too luxurious.

On the rare occasions when he was at home, he continued his practice of consolidation, most notably codifying and humanizing (by the abolition of torture) a pretty haphazard legal system.* He also found time to build the most stupendous villa for himself (an estate of more than 66 acres containing a hundred buildings, many copied from things he had seen on his travels) at Tivoli, just outside Rome, and to commission the Pantheon (see page 126). He had a lover named Antinous, who died young and whom Hadrian subsequently deified (generally frowned upon, but not as bad as making your horse consul, see page 93).

Antoninus Pius (138–161): A fairly uneventful time, but worth mentioning because the Antonine Wall in Scotland is named after him. When Hadrian died, the Senate, which had never forgiven him for the executions mentioned above, tried to prevent him from being made into a god. (Emperors were always made into gods after they died. That was considered absolutely fine.) Antoninus persuaded them to change their mind, which is probably how he earned the nickname Pius.

Marcus Aurelius (161–180): The last of the five good emperors; was also a philosopher and is dealt with on page 170, as is his far-from-good successor, Commodus.

---

* A much later emperor, Justinian, completely revised Roman law, but drew heavily on Hadrian's reforms.

Then followed a number of emperors who have been all but forgotten, including a period of half a century when no one lasted much more than two years. Memorable figures from the later empire are few:

Diocletian (284–305): By this time the empire was not only being torn apart by internal wars and attacks from external tribes; it was also suffering from galloping inflation and was in a financial and administrative mess. How very modern of it. Diocletian finally decided that it was too much for one man to rule and divided the empire in two. He took charge of the eastern part and his friend Maximian took the west.

Constantine the Great (306–337): The one who became a Christian and made Christianity acceptable throughout the Roman world. He also brought the empire back together again, defeating Licinius, who was by that time in charge in the east, and making himself sole emperor. But the damage was done. Constantine made Byzantium (modern Istanbul) his capital, rebuilding it and renaming it Constantinople, and the focus of the empire moved to the east. While Rome remained prestigious and wealthy, it would never again be the political center of the universe.

Rome was finally invaded and sacked by a Germanic tribe called the **Visigoths**, led by **Alaric**, in 410.* Although

---

* You can't mention Alaric the Goth without a quick word on Attila the Hun. Attila came a little later (he died in 453), but he, too, rampaged over the Roman Empire, invading all sorts of places from the Balkans to Gaul. He eventually murdered his brother and became the sort of autocratic ruler that has made his name a byword.

Constantinople went from strength to strength, this date ("the Fall of Rome") is normally regarded as the end of the Roman Empire.[*]

About Roman historians

Julius Caesar (*ca.* 100–44 B.C.) chronicled his own conquests of Gaul, famously beginning *Gallia est omnis divisa in partes tres*—"All of Gaul is divided into three parts" (see page 74)—and it doesn't get much more exciting than that. The books are mostly straight military history, with some useful historical information on Gaul and its people and perhaps just a glancing reference to what a great general Caesar was.

Most people know of **Livy** (59 B.C.–A.D. 17), perhaps because he wrote 142 books of history and told us practically everything we know about everything that happened *ab urbe condita* (see page 72) to the early years of Augustus. He covered the period of the kingdom, the wars with Carthage, wars in the east, all sorts of stuff about Marius and Sulla, Caesar's invasion of Gaul and his civil war against Pompey—you name it. But he wasn't an accurate historian. Really what he was doing was praising the ancient Roman character and virtues, as opposed to the decadence of his own times. Personally I could never get along with him,

---

[*] Actually the last Roman emperor in the West wasn't deposed until A.D. 476, but despite his fancy-sounding name—Romulus Augustulus—no one was taking much notice by then.

not because I am a stickler for historical accuracy but because he had a Henry James–like attitude about the length of sentences and paragraphs, and by the time you came to the verb at the end, you had lost all trace of the noun at the beginning.

But give me **Tacitus** (*ca.* A.D. 55–A.D. 117) anytime. His *Annals* and *Histories* start with the reign of Tiberius and go up to his own time, so they include Caligula, Nero and all the fun people who went really off the rails. Tacitus was sharp on character analysis and a superb writer, but what makes him so enjoyable is that he was pretty opposed to the whole concept of emperors, so he tended to believe (and relate) all the bad stuff about them—and there was no shortage of that.

Suetonius (*ca.* A.D. 70–*ca.* A.D. 140) is more a gossip than a historian, so great fun if you are not looking for scholarly rigor. His *Lives of the Caesars* covers Julius and the first eleven emperors, up to Domitian. If what you want to know is that Augustus was careless about his dress, frugal in his eating habits and had eyebrows that met in the middle, or that Nero played with little ivory horses and chariots even after he became emperor, Suetonius is your man.

6

The Posh Stuff:
Classical Literature

The one person we've all heard of in Greek literature is
Homer, who may not have existed or may have been two
people.* But worrying about that is like worrying about
whether Bacon or Marlowe wrote Shakespeare's plays:
Frankly, who cares, they're great stuff, sit back and enjoy.
After Homer there is a bit of a blank for a few hundred years,
and then we hit a Golden Age in Athens (which you know
about already if you've read Chapter 4).

Homer and other Greek literary figures

Homer (probably ninth century B.C.) wrote two great epics, the
Iliad and the *Odyssey*, almost certainly based on existing ballads.†
The story behind the *Iliad* is that Helen was the most beautiful
woman in the world and lots of Greek noblemen were after her.

---

* One of the things people do think they know about him is that he was blind,
although as there is debate about whether or not he existed at all, this seems to
come under the heading of "surmise."

† Another thing people think they know about Homer is that he didn't actually
write anything; his stories were circulated by word of mouth and only written
down centuries later—by someone else.

She married Menelaus, King of Sparta, but all the rejected suitors made a promise that they would come to her rescue should anyone abduct her (a sort of early pre-nup in reverse). And guess what?

Yes, she ran off with Paris, a prince of Troy (see page 42 for the story of the Judgment of Paris that started it all). And all the Greek warriors, including Achilles, Agamemnon, Odysseus (Ulysses in Latin), and Ajax, trotted off and camped outside Troy for ten years to try to get her back.

All this happens before the *Iliad* begins (Ilium or Ilion is the other name for Troy, by the way, hence the title). What mostly happens in the *Iliad* is that Achilles has a hissy fit because Agamemnon has stolen a slave girl of his, sulks in his tent for eight books and spends the ninth telling Agamemnon he's had enough and he's going home. Achilles is a great warrior, so the war is going badly for the Greeks because of his petulance. Achilles's friend Patroclus borrows his armor, goes out to fight on his behalf and is promptly killed by the Trojan prince Hector. Achilles finally bursts out of his tent, kills Hector and turns the tide of the battle. There is no mention here of the Trojan horse; that story crops up in the *Odyssey* but isn't told in detail until Virgil's *Aeneid*, so we'll come to it in about a thousand years' time (see page 113).

So, at long last, the Greeks win and set out for home. But Odysseus takes another ten years to do it, seven of them dallying with the goddess Calypso, during which time he's presumably ignoring his wife Penelope's text messages asking him to pick up a couple of bottles of retsina wine on his way past the liquor store. This is where the *Odyssey* begins: Penelope has been besieged by suitors urging her to marry again on the basis that her husband is surely dead. She delays a decision, saying that she will choose one of them once she has finished a piece of weaving, which she works at during the day and then secretly unravels at night.

Zeus orders Calypso to release Odysseus, but on the next leg of the journey he is shipwrecked. (Poseidon doesn't like him because he has blinded the god's son, the Cyclops Polyphemus—yet another example of how easy and how foolhardy it is to upset Poseidon.) Odysseus is now rescued by a princess called Nausicaa. In her father's palace he recounts the events of his journey: his visit to the land of the Lotus-Eaters (there's a poem by Tennyson about this); his visit to the land of the Cyclops (who by the way had only one eye each and now have a high-tech Wimbledon line-judge named after them); his encounter with the sorceress Circe, who turns his companions into pigs; his descent into the Underworld, where he meets many dead companions; his struggles with Scylla and Charybdis (see page 43)—and on and on and on. Can't you just see the nice people in the palace yawning and wishing they'd left him stranded on the beach so they could go to bed?

Anyway. Odysseus gets home to discover that the suitors are eating him out of house and home, but that Penelope is going to make her choice the next day. He wins the contest Penelope has set for the suitors, kills them all and they live happily ever after. If she has a few harsh words to say because he has been away chasing after other women for twenty years, Homer doesn't mention it.

About Troy

For many years, scholars believed that the city of **Troy** was no more than the basis for the mythical events described in the *Iliad*. But in 1871 the obsession of a self-made German millionaire, **Heinrich Schliemann**, proved them wrong.

Schliemann had fallen in love with the *Iliad* as a child and was convinced that it was a historical account. Homer's writings gave him sufficient information to set up an archaeological dig in northwestern Turkey. Schliemann was no archaeologist and didn't know or care about digging very gently in case you disturbed anything; he also wasn't interested in anything that didn't tie in with his own theories. Despite his bull-in-a-china-shop methods, more delicate digging has since confirmed that a fortified city—or rather a succession of nine cities, one on top of the other—had existed just where Homer said it did, from about 3000 B.C. to A.D. 400. The second layer from the bottom—known as Troy II—had been destroyed by fire, tying in with Homer's account, but scholars now think that the sixth or seventh layer is probably the one that dates from the right period.

But Homer was of course not the only literary figure in ancient Greece...

Sappho (probably seventh century B.C.): The only female writer of classical times whose name means anything to most of us. She lived on the island of Lesbos, surrounded by a community of women, but it is likely that this was for the sake of studying music and poetry rather than for anything, well, sapphic. That said, whether she was thinking of men or women, the fragments of poetry that have come down to us contain some pretty sexy stuff.

Aesop (*ca.* 620–560 B.C.): Wrote fables—stories about animals, with a moral. There are lots of them, but perhaps the most famous are *The Hare and the Tortoise* (slow and steady wins the race) and *The Fox and the Grapes* (in which the grapes are too high up for the fox to reach them, so he turns away, sniffing "I'm sure they are sour"—hence the expression "sour grapes"). Warnings against a wolf in sheep's clothing and the foolishness of killing a goose that lays golden eggs also come from Aesop.

Aeschylus (*ca.* 525–456 B.C.): The first of the three great tragedians of Athens, known as "the father of Greek tragedy" and author of, among others, *Seven Against Thebes* and the *Oresteia* trilogy, *Agamemnon*, *Choephoroe* and *Eumenides*. The story of the *Oresteia* is—roughly—that many years ago, Agamemnon, on his way to Troy, agreed to sacrifice his daughter Iphigenia to the goddess Artemis (Diana in latin) in return for good sailing weather. In some versions Artemis took pity on the girl and saved her, but even so Agamemnon's wife Clytemnestra never forgave him. So she murders her husband on his return from Troy. Their son Orestes in turn kills his mother and is pursued by the Furies (a.k.a. Eumenides; see page 36), who are stirred into action by the ghost of Clytemnestra. The issue is taken to the court of Athena, and Orestes is acquitted. The Choephoroe, by the way, are the women, including Orestes's sister Electra—who pour libations (sacrificial wine) on Agamemnon's tomb.

Sophocles (496–406 B.C.): Came to the fore after he beat Aeschylus in a drama contest in 468 B.C., when doubtless he was the Angry Young Man of Greek tragedy. His great surviving plays are *Oedipus the King, Oedipus at Colonus* and *Antigone*. Oedipus is the one immortalized in song by Tom Lehrer ("His name appears in Freud's index/'Cause he loved his mother"). He is abandoned and left to die as a baby because of a prophecy that he would kill his father and marry his mother, but—as always when people try to get around prophecies like this—he is rescued by a kindly shepherd or some such person,[*] and brought up by people he assumes are his natural parents. In due course he bumps into his father and, not recognizing him (it's been awhile), quarrels with and kills him. He then goes on to the city of Thebes, which is being hassled by the Sphinx and her riddles. Oedipus solves the riddle,[†] relieves the city and marries the queen, Jocasta, who just happens to be a teeny bit older than he is…

…and four children later, word gets out that Jocasta is his mother. She hangs herself and Oedipus blinds himself (according to Sophocles, using Jocasta's brooch. Yuck).

---

[*] Just to be sure that he would die, they pushed a spike through his feet, hence the name Oedipus, which means "swollen foot." But they had not counted on the kindly shepherd.

[†] What goes on four legs in the morning, two legs at noon and three legs in the evening? Answer: man—as we were allowed to say in those days—who crawls as a baby, walks upright most of his life and ends up leaning on a stick.

That is the background and action of *Oedipus the King*. The remaining two plays deal with Oedipus in banishment, tended by his daughter Antigone, and the subsequent destruction of his family. More corpses than *Hamlet* by the end of it all.

Euripides (*ca.* 480–406 B.C.): His plays *Orestes*, *Electra* and *Iphigenia at Aulis* cover the stories described under Aeschylus above, though in this version no one intervenes to save Iphigenia. Perhaps Euripides's most famous play is *Medea*, about the lady who murders her own children to avenge herself on their father, Jason (see page 44), who has abandoned her. Powerful stuff, especially if you happen to have seen Diana Rigg doing it, but see also page 154 for the philosophical aspect.

Aristophanes (*ca.* 448–*ca.* 388 B.C.): The only comic dramatist of the period whose work survives. His plays include *The Clouds*, *The Birds*, *Frogs* and, most memorably, *Lysistrata*, which is the one where the women on both sides of a conflict between Athens and Sparta refuse to have sex with their husbands until they end the war. *The Oxford Companion to Classical Literature* remarks austerely that "as results from part of the theme of the comedy, there are passages of gross indecency," which may be why the play appeals to modern audiences who don't give a hoot about wars between Athens and Sparta.

The classical theater

Now here's an odd thing. The great classical work of literary theory is **Aristotle**'s *Poetics*, though all the great Greek tragedians were dead before Aristotle was born. But hey, that's Aristotle all over: not inventing, but classifying and organizing. We'll be hearing lots more about him in later chapters.

The *Poetics* deals mostly with tragedy, of which, Aristotle says, the plot is "the first principle, and, as it were, the soul of a tragedy; character holds the second place."

What Aristotle wants is "unity of action"—a single thread running through the entire work: The hero has (or achieves) success, makes a mistake, suffers a reversal and then, in all probability, tears his eyes out or is driven mad by the Furies. This is not the same as "unity of hero": The *Odyssey* may be all about Odysseus, but it wanders around all over the place, in more senses than one. For the audience, what matters is to experience pity and fear, "effecting the proper purging of these emotions." In other words, if you come out of the theater feeling drained, you've gotten your money's worth.

The hero of a tragedy should not be a pre-eminently good or bad man, because although the misfortunes of the one or the downfall of the other might satisfy some moral sense, neither would evoke pity or fear. So the central figure of a tragedy is one "whose misfortune is brought about not by vice or depravity, but by some error or frailty."

The *Poetics* had a great influence on later European drama: Macbeth's "vaulting ambition" and Othello's loving "not wisely but too well" are just the sort of frailty Aristotle was talking about. On the other hand, Shakespeare didn't stick rigidly to unity of action—Edmund's affairs with both Goneril and Regan in *King Lear* must be considered a subplot, and Aristotle might have thought Rosencrantz and Guildenstern were surplus to requirements, too. The French classical tragedians, however, notably Corneille and Racine, not only stuck to unity of action but went a stage further: They introduced unities of time and place, so that the action of the play took place within a period of twenty-four hours (the purists insisted on "real time," i.e., no more than a couple of hours) and all in the same scene. The extreme example is Corneille's *Le Cid*, in which the hero has to defeat a vast Moorish army—off-stage—in the course of a single night in order to make the play fit the rules.

Aristotle's rules aside, Greek drama, whether tragedy or comedy, followed a fairly set pattern. It began with a prologue—an idea borrowed by Shakespeare for *Romeo and Juliet* and Frankie Howerd for *Up Pompeii!**—followed by the entrance of the chorus, then the action of the play, interspersed with commentary from the chorus. Early plays had a lot of chorus and little action; by the time of Sophocles *et al.*, individual actors had become more important, but the chorus was still there to provide a few tunes and point out the moral.

The plays always had a religious background, so very often a god was brought on at the end to sort things out. The actor playing the god was carried by a crane (*mechane* in Greek,

---

* Mentioning *Up Pompeii!* gives me an excuse to bring in the word *innuendo*, which comes from a Latin gerund or verbal noun, meaning "that which must be conveyed by a nod."

machina in Latin) to give the impression that he was descending from the sky. Hence the expression *deus ex machina*—"a god from a machine"—to mean some unexpected intervention that resolves an apparently hopeless situation. A classical variation on "with one bound he was free."

The Romans weren't as hot on theater as the Greeks, and a lot of Roman plays are adapted from Greek originals. **Seneca the Younger** (*ca.* 4 B.C.–A.D. 65, see page 155) wrote tragedies, **Plautus** (*ca.* 254–184 B.C.) produced some raunchy, crowd-pleasing comedies (Frankie Howerd quoted him a lot too), and **Terence** (*ca.* 190–159 B.C.) wrote comedies for a more refined audience, but for the most part the Romans seem to have preferred chariot races and people being torn apart. See Chapter 10 for more about that.

Roman literature

After Aristotle we can skip forward a few hundred years to the **Golden Age** of Roman literature. If you look at the dates—and see Cicero on page 111 and the historians on page 99—you can see why it was called a Golden Age: Practically everyone you have heard of was born within a couple of generations of each other.

Catullus (*ca.* 84–54 B.C.) addressed his best poetry to a lady he called Lesbia. This was meant to be a compliment, likening her to the poet Sappho, who lived on Lesbos (see page 104); Lesbia's real name was Clodia, and she was the sister (and some say lover) of the Clodius mentioned under Cicero. Whether or not she slept with her brother, Clodia did sleep with a lot of other people and gave Catullus a rotten time—as a result of which he wrote some beautiful, passionate poetry, so it's an ill wind...

About Cicero

It's difficult to know where to put **Cicero**—politics, literature, even philosophy—so let's give him a box of his own.

Born in 106 B.C., he studied law and made his first great speech at the age of twenty-seven, successfully defending one Sextus Roscius on a charge of parricide (killing one's parent). This brought him fame as an advocate; at the same time he started moving up the political ladder, becoming consul in 63 B.C. He then foiled a revolutionary plot by a corrupt patrician called Catilina, which produced some of his greatest speeches (*In Catilinam*). This was a time of great political in-fighting in Rome, and Cicero, who was notoriously pleased with himself and had a habit of making enemies, fell out big time with the unscrupulous but influential Clodius and to a lesser extent with Julius Caesar, and found himself exiled. Caesar forgave him a year later and Cicero returned to Rome to continued success as an advocate, a position that was consolidated after Clodius was murdered (which had only been a matter of time).

Cicero then sided with Pompey during the civil war (see page 83), but was again pardoned by Caesar and was able to live peacefully in Rome until the latter's assassination.

Cicero was a staunch defender of the republic and although he admired Caesar the man, he was horrified at the power he wielded, and even more horrified at the additional power that Rome wanted to give him. For much of this he blamed Mark Antony; his late great speeches, the *Philippics*, are diatribes against Antony and his policies. There are fourteen *Philippics*, so Antony can have been in little doubt of Cicero's views. Antony had Cicero murdered in 43 B.C., and his head and hands were displayed on the Rostra, the platform in the Forum from which orators addressed the people.

For a bit more about Cicero's speeches, see page 162. He also wrote works of philosophy and books about oratory and kept up a remarkably frank lifelong correspondence with his friend Atticus, which gives great insight into his own vanity, wavering moods and political indecision. He wrote and wrote and wrote: It is no surprise that his secretary Tiro should be credited with having invented shorthand. He was pompous, fantastically fond of the sound of his own voice and tireless in the pursuit of his own ambition. But he died because he wouldn't give up on his own ideals of liberty, and you can't make cheap jokes about that.

Virgil (70–19 B.C.): Author of the great Latin epic, the *Aeneid*, the story of how the Trojan prince Aeneas escapes from Troy and makes it to Italy to found Rome. Taking a break from his journey in Carthage (see page 78), he becomes involved with the queen, Dido, and tells her about the fall of Troy and his journey so far. This is where the details of the Trojan Horse come from (see *Homer*, page 101): The war was at a deadlock and one of the Greeks—possibly Odysseus, he was normally the one with the bright ideas—suggested that they build an enormous wooden horse and then withdraw from the siege, leaving behind a man named Sinon. Sinon would go to the Trojans pretending to be a traitor and giving them the horse as an offering to Athena (who had not hitherto been on the Trojans' side, having been passed over in the Golden Apple awards; see page 42). The Trojans fell for it, bless them, not realizing that the horse was full of soldiers who would leap out at night once the horse was inside the walls, and sack the city.

Other key events of the *Aeneid* are Aeneas's desertion of Dido—he abandons her after being scolded by the gods for dallying in Carthage when his destiny is to get off his backside and found Rome, and she commits suicide—and his descent into the Underworld to meet his dead father (see page 30). The rest is about his arrival in Italy and his (surely not unexpected) war with the people who are already there. Frankly this second half goes on a bit, but in the end Aeneas wins, marries the local king's daughter and is all set to be the ancestor of the Romans (see *Romulus and Remus*, page 71).

Virgil also wrote a collection of pastoral poems called *Eclogues*, and a long poem called *Georgics*, about farming and with advice on raising crops, rearing cattle, bee-keeping and planting herbs on land unfit for anything else. Who said the classics were no use to anyone nowadays?

Horace (65–8 B.C.): Mostly wrote odes, but also a longer poem called *Ars Poetica*—"On the Art of Poetry"—which includes the famous words (I'm translating loosely here) "Even the great Homer sometimes has an off day." Lots of Latin "tags" come from Horace: *nil desperandum* ("never despair"), *carpe diem* ("seize the day") and the one that First World War poet Wilfred Owen called "the old lie," *dulce et decorum est pro patria mori* ("it is sweet and honorable to die for one's country"). Horace's poems are full of robust common sense, advocating moderation and simple pleasures, with the occasional glass of good red wine thrown in. *Nunc est bibendum* ("now is the time for drinking," motto of many an oenophile society) is also one of his.

Ovid (43 B.C.–A.D. 18): Lived in fashionable circles at the time of Augustus, so it was almost inevitable that he should have an affair with the Emperor's daughter Julia (everyone else did), as a result of which he spent the last ten years of his life in exile in a gloomy area near the Black Sea. Actually, the part about Julia may be scurrilous rumor; Ovid himself seems to have thought that he was exiled because he wrote a poem called *Ars Amatoria* ("The Art of Love"), a racy guide to promiscuity and adulterous "love," written in a mock-serious elegiac form. Something in it to offend everyone, particularly the rather prudish Augustus.

Chief among Ovid's other works is the *Metamorphoses*, an important source of our knowledge of ancient myths. He focused on stories in which one of the protagonists ended up turning into an animal, plant or other non-human form. You might think this was a specialist area, but he got fifteen books out of it. The *Metamorphoses* contains the stories of Pyramus and Thisbe, which later turn up in Shakespeare's *A Midsummer Night's Dream* (the "metamorphosis" in the original is that a mulberry tree grows from the blood of the dead lovers); Echo and Narcissus (Narcissus rejects the love of Echo, and in punishment Aphrodite makes him fall in love with his own reflection in a fountain; he pines away and turns into the flower that bears his name); and Arachne, who challenged Athena to a weaving contest and ended up being turned into a spider. There are lots more, but you get the gist.

Pliny the Elder (*ca.* 23–79 A.D.): Incredibly prolific, but his main contribution to posterity is a massive work of what he called natural history, but which covers much more than we understand by that term. Its thirty-seven books (!) cover the composition of the universe, geography, zoology, botany (including a lot of the medicinal properties of plants), metallurgy and lots more.

Pliny's nephew, known as **Pliny the Younger** (61 or 62–*ca.* 113 A.D.), wrote volumes and volumes of letters that tell us a lot about the life of a wealthy Roman during this comparatively placid period of the empire. Toward the end of his life, he became governor of the province of Bithynia, now part of Turkey. His final book of *Letters* contains those addressed from Bithynia to the Emperor Trajan, asking advice on many trivial matters and showing how very hands-on the central government of the empire was at this time. But Pliny also consulted the emperor on what he was to do with a group of Christians who had been denounced to him: If a man had "repented" of being a Christian, could he be excused, or did having once committed the offense tarnish him forever? Trajan replied that such a person could be forgiven, provided he went back to worshipping the right gods, but he also came down hard on the idea of anonymous informers: "For this is both a dangerous kind of precedent and out of keeping with the spirit of our age."

Juvenal (*ca.* 55–130 A.D.): His *Satires* were so, shall we say, earthy that my school edition was censored. It was one of those books where the lines were numbered and sometimes it skipped from line twenty to line forty, and you knew that you were missing the part about it being more difficult to get an erection as you got older. In fact, Juvenal was a harsh moralist, and his theme is really the vice and depravity to which Rome had sunk by this time. What he's saying is that it is crazy to pray for a long life, because of all the indignities that go with age, including it being more difficult... You get my drift. The maxim *Mens sana in corpore sano*—"a healthy mind in a healthy body"—comes later in the same poem. Juvenal is known to have influenced lots of English writers who later wrote raunchy and/or satirical stuff, including Chaucer, Donne, Swift, Pope and Samuel Johnson.

7

The Fancy Stuff: Architecture and Art

We all know what classical buildings look like. They're those big chunky things with lots of columns, and they're all over the place. The White House, the Pentagon and the Capitol in Washington, D.C., the National Gallery and Somerset House in London; most of the city of Bath, England; and almost every civic building in the Western world that is over a hundred years old. They are all inspired by the designs established by the Greeks well over two thousand years ago.

As in many cultures, the oldest buildings we know about are temples, for the simple reason that anything built to honor the gods was more important than anything built to house mere mortals, and therefore made to last. As early as the seventh century B.C., the Greeks (following the example of the Egyptians) were using stone for temples; by the sixth century they were using it for public buildings as well.

Doric, Ionic and Corinthian

There are three principal styles or orders of classical architecture, defined largely by the type of **column** they use and more specifically by the style of the top (properly called the **capital**, which is the part that joins the column to whatever it is supporting, the **entablature**). Such things as the ratio of the diameter of the column to its height (1:6 in the purest Doric form) and the distance that each column stood from the next went a long way toward dictating the proportions of the whole building.

The oldest and simplest of these orders is the **Doric**, which emerged on mainland Greece. The Dorians were an ancient people who had settled in the Peloponnese some time before the beginning of this book. Ethnically the Spartans were Dorians, so it'll come as no surprise that the Doric column is sturdy with no adornment and, in the early days, no base.

The fancier **Ionic**—originating in Asia Minor, where all the decadence came from*—is slimmer and has four spiral scrolls on the capital. These two orders were kept strictly separate for a couple of hundred years (this was the time when the mainland Greeks were fighting the Persians for control of the Greek-speaking towns in Ionia, so it's not surprising that an "us and them" attitude spilled over into architecture). By Hellenistic times this had relaxed a little, so that the styles were allowed to develop: Doric columns tended to become

---

* Well, that's what the Spartans thought, anyway. See the footnote on page 66 about the Persians using arrows.

slimmer and more widely spaced, creating less severe buildings that let in more light. The two styles occasionally even appeared on the same building. Purists maintained that this was heresy, but—a bit like those of us who still argue in favor of the apostrophe—they had to accept that they weren't going to win every battle.

The time was ripe for the emergence of the third great order, the **Corinthian**. If you have ever had occasion to read a gardening book that mentions the cottage-garden plant called bear's breeches, you will know that its opulent leaves inspired the design of the Corinthian capital. (The plant's Latin name is *Acanthus mollis*, but it wouldn't have been called that even in Roman times, because it wasn't the Romans who invented Latin names for plants as we know them.)

Anyway, the Corinthian order was generally a lot fancier than anything that had gone before and reflected the "art for art's sake" attitude that was a feature of the Hellenistic world.*

The Romans adopted and adapted these architectural orders, introducing two of their own—the **Tuscan**, which was their equivalent of the Doric, and the **Composite**, which was basically a mixture of the Ionic and the Corinthian. Why these names haven't caught on in the same way as the Greek ones is a matter for speculation for anyone who cares to speculate about it.

---

* Sparta had ceased to be a force to be reckoned with by this time. The concept of "art for art's sake" would really have been Greek to them.

If you want to see these columns *in situ*, the Parthenon and the Temple of Hephaestus, both in Athens, are good for Doric, or there is a lovely temple at Segesta in Sicily; many of the Deep South plantation houses of the Antebellum style have Ionic ones; and the Pantheon in Rome and the Capitol in Washington, D.C., have Corinthian columns.

About the Seven Wonders of the World

The **Seven Wonders of the Ancient World**, chosen by an otherwise forgotten Greek poet called Antipater of Sidon in the second century B.C. as being "remarkable for their splendor or magnitude," were:

- **The Hanging Gardens of Babylon**
- **The Mausoleum of Halicarnassus**
- **The Pharos** (lighthouse) **of Alexandria**
- **The Colossus of Rhodes**
- **The Temple of Artemis at Ephesus**
- **The Statue of Zeus at Olympia**
- **The Great Pyramid of Cheops** (or **Khufu**)

Of the seven, only the pyramid is still in existence, but there is talk about rebuilding the Colossus—a gigantic statue of the sun god Helios—at the entrance to Rhodes harbor. The original was toppled by an earthquake, and the plan is that, rather than attempting to replicate it, the architect will create a massive light sculpture. The mind boggles.

On a more banal note, the ruins of the Mausoleum are just outside Bodrum in Turkey, and if you drive there from Istanbul or Izmir, you pass what is left of the Temple of Artemis on the way. The temple was vandalized and rebuilt a number of times over the centuries, before being destroyed for the last time in an act of anti-pagan violence by Christians in around A.D. 400. The Statue of Zeus was probably destroyed by fire or earthquake, but no one seems to be sure. The Pharos of Alexandria was weakened by a series of earthquakes, but lasted into the Middle Ages.

Oh, and it is just possible that the Hanging Gardens of Babylon never existed at all. If they did, there is a rather sweet story attached to them. Babylon, for all its magnificence (and it was the most magnificent city in the world at one time), was flat and arid. King Nebuchadnezzar was married to a lady who came from a green and mountainous place and he created a vast, terraced garden to make her feel less homesick. Aww. Impressively, given that this was the sixth century B.C., he installed a pump that brought water from the River Euphrates all the way up to the top of the artificial hillside so that it could irrigate the plants on its way down. And yes, it is the same Nebuchadnezzar who appears in the Old Testament, gaining notoriety for destroying Jerusalem.

Some important buildings

There are remnants of Greek temples all over the place. In addition to the one that became a wonder of the world (see page 132), there is the fantastic **Temple of Apollo** in Didyma, in southwestern Turkey. It took something like 700 years to build, ran monumentally over budget and was never actually completed. *Didyma* means "twins," and this temple is not a million miles from the **Temple of Artemis** (Apollo's twin sister) at Ephesus. It was 360 feet (110 m) long with over 120 (mostly Ionic) columns, each intended to be almost sixty-five feet (20 m) high. It's an impressive ruin by any standards, but its real selling point is that there is a scale drawing of the temple scratched into a marble wall; the architects knew it was going to take more than a lifetime to build and wanted the next generation to know what the plan was. Ironically, if the temple had ever been finished, this would have been polished over and lost forever. Another ill wind, eh?

Most people nowadays would say that the most important building in ancient Greece was the **Parthenon** in Athens. Certainly it is the most iconic, using *iconic* in the sense of "we all know what it looks like." So let's give it a moment or two.

First off, the Parthenon is not the same as the **Acropolis**; it is *part* of the Acropolis. *Acropolis* means "high town," and Athens, like many historic towns all over the world, was built on a hill or rocky plateau that was difficult to attack. So the word has come to mean the citadel—the central, usually fortified, part of the city where the important religious and civic buildings were. It was all rebuilt under the auspices of Pericles after the Persians destroyed Athens (see page 56), and the Parthenon—a temple dedicated to Athena, but also a symbol of the invincibility of the Athenians—is the most important of a number of buildings that survive.* It only ever had forty-six outer columns, about 36 feet (11 m) high—no big deal by Didyma and Ephesus standards—but it was dedicated to the most important goddess of the most important city in the world, so deserves some respect. It is also a highly sophisticated piece of architecture in that it allows for some oddities in our visual perception. For example, to counteract "imperfections" caused by optical illusions and the laws of perspective, the Parthenon's base slopes downward very slightly at the corners, and the columns lean ever so slightly inward.

The Parthenon was, like many important buildings of the period, sculpted all over. There were ninety-two panels (called **metopes**) along the **architrave** (the bit just above the columns, part of the **entablature**); sculptures on the **pediments** (the triangular gable-like parts at either end) and over 492 feet (150 m) of **friezes** around the central chamber, all carved with stories about the gods and Athenian victories over various enemies. The chamber also contained a 42-foot (13-m) gold and ivory statue of Athena.†

---

* Other buildings of the Acropolis included an *asclepieion*—see page 139.

† The original statue had disappeared by A.D. 400, but a replica exists in a replica of the Parthenon in, of all places, Nashville, Tennessee.

So all in all, the place was well worth looting. Which is why you can see chunks of it in the British Museum. In the early nineteenth century, Greece was controlled by the Turks, who were allies of the British in the war against Napoleon. A certain Lord Elgin was the British Ambassador to Turkey and inveigled the Turks into giving him permission to take a few souvenirs. Whether they realized he was going to hack off big chunks of marble is a cornerstone of the debate that has raged ever since as to whether or not the so-called Elgin Marbles should be "sent home."

Roman buildings

You could write a whole book about the fabulous buildings in Rome—indeed, plenty of people have. Here is a note about just two of the most remarkable.

The first **Pantheon** in Rome was built in 27 B.C. to commemorate Octavian's victory over Antony and Cleopatra at the Battle of Actium a few years earlier. The current version was commissioned by Hadrian (he of the wall—see page 96) in the second century A.D. The name means that it is dedicated to all (*pan*) the gods (*theos*),* although it became a Christian church in A.D. 609 (the first pagan temple to be taken over in this way).

It is remarkable in all sorts of ways. Mostly because it is nearly 2,000 years old and has survived virtually intact, so it is

---

* Yes, both of those words do come from Greek rather than Latin.

probably the best-preserved building of its age in the world. Its height, 142 feet (43.3 m), is the same as the diameter of its dome, which makes it "feel" perfect the moment you walk in. Until the twentieth century it was the largest vault ever built, and it remains the largest unreinforced concrete dome, weighing over 4,960 tons. When the door is closed, the only light comes from a massive hole in the ceiling called the *oculus* ("eye"), which also acts as a sundial, telling the time and doing clever things with equinoxes and solstices. And, just in case you are wondering, the floor slopes gently toward a central drain, so that any rain that comes in quickly flows away. In other words, it is just amazing.

So is the **Colosseum**, which dates from about fifty years earlier and is the largest Roman amphitheater ever built. Although not on a par with the Pantheon, it is still in pretty good condition and you can see that, as so often, the Romans thought of everything when they built it. It was four stories high, decorated with Doric, Ionic and Corinthian columns, had a huge awning to keep the sun off the more important members of the audience, and could accommodate 50,000 people. The seats were steeply banked so that—and I am not making this up—*everyone could see:* an innovation that many modern theaters should really consider next time they have a makeover. Numbered arches made it easy to find your seat.

All this was supported by eighty walls that radiated from the arena. (The name comes from the Latin word for sand, *harena*, because the area was scattered with sand after each round of combat to soak up the blood.) Beneath the wooden floor of the arena was a network of cages, rooms and passageways for the people and animals that took part in the "games" (more about them on page 165), plus lifts and trapdoors to get them up into the arena. A fence about 5 feet (1.5 m) high separated the arena from the lowest tier of spectators and was topped with wooden rollers to stop the wild beasts climbing over it.

The Colosseum was also a masterpiece of crowd control. A system of corridors called—rather too graphically perhaps—**vomitoria** opened out into the tiers of seats. Each efficiently "spewed" its section of the crowd into their places and equally effectively vomited them out into the streets at the end of the performance. It is said that the Colosseum could be emptied in a quarter of an hour.*

Amphitheaters caught on in a big way after the Colosseum opened and some are remarkably well preserved. The one in Verona is still used for spectacular opera productions and the one in Arles for bullfights.

On a smaller scale

It's worth a quick mention here of the private house of a wealthy Roman, because some of the terms they used are still familiar. By the fourth century B.C., Rome

---

* Contrary to rumor, there was never a room—in a Roman house or anywhere else—called a *vomitorium*. If you wanted to throw up after overindulging at a banquet, you went outside with everyone else.

had become very crowded, and building technology involving a sort of concrete made from volcanic ash allowed the Romans to erect high-rise apartment buildings to house the poor.

However, those who could afford it had more luxurious homes in town and probably villas in the country as well. Obviously there were variations on the basic theme, but most such houses were built around a central **atrium**, wholly or partly open to the sky, and a **peristyle**—a covered colonnade a bit like a cloister. Entrance to the house was through a **vestibule**; the atrium acted as a reception room; bedrooms, dining areas, kitchens, etc. were built off it. The dining room was known as the **triclinium**, because couches were arranged on three sides of the central dining table. Diners reclined, three to a couch, while eating, and there was a strict protocol about who lay where.

About the Forum

Originally the marketplace in a large Roman town, the **forum** developed into the focus of political, religious and social life. All the main civic buildings surrounded it, debates took place inside it, and important public notices were posted there. The main Forum in Rome (known as the **Forum Romanum**, imaginatively enough) contains the remains of the Curia or Senate House, the Rostra from which speeches were made,

---

the House of the Vestals, various temples and the triumphal arches of Titus and a later emperor, Septimius Severus. It's open to the public, and it's free, which means that you can wander in at lunchtime and have your sandwiches within inches of where Julius Caesar was murdered or Cicero made his greatest speeches. Or you can say, "It's just a pile of old ruins," and go to McDonald's.

A bit of etymology: The word *forensic* comes from *forum*, because the forum was the focus of so many things to do with the law. The Greek equivalent was the *agora*, whence the word *agoraphobic*, meaning "afraid of open spaces." And Septimius Severus won his great victory over the Parthians, a people of southwest Asia who could twist around in the saddle and fire their arrows backward while they were retreating—hence the expression "a Parthian shot," meaning a final remark to which the hearer has no chance of replying. Most people would now say "a parting shot," because they're a bit vague about who the Parthians were, so there's a chance for you to show off at dinner parties.

Finally, a bit about triumphal arches. They were freestanding monuments—as opposed to being built into a wall and serving as an entrance—erected to celebrate an emperor's victory in battle. A triumph—that is, a triumphal procession—had, in Republican times, been a serious thing, awarded by the Senate to a victorious general. He could then put on a laurel wreath and a gold-trimmed robe and parade through the streets of Rome at the head of his army, displaying his prisoners and the spoils of war, accompanied by trumpeters and other musicians and generally making no secret of the fact that he had done something to shout about. Later on, you won't be surprised to learn, emperors awarded triumphs to themselves because they felt like it. And presumably built themselves arches for similar self-aggrandizing reasons. The other great surviving arch is Constantine's, near the Colosseum. Like those of Titus and Septimius Severus, it may not have led anywhere, but that doesn't stop it from being pretty impressive.

Greek art

Sculpture was the great classical art form, predating even architecture: The Greeks first made images of the gods, then built temples to house them. But lots of even more ancient people produced sculptures. In Egypt, Ramses the Great was having colossal statues of himself built in the thirteenth century B.C., 400 years before Homer. What really made the Greeks stand out from the crowd was their **vase painting**.

They did this in Crete way back in time, but the art died out when the Minoan civilization collapsed. It is likely that there were still skilled craftsmen farther east—among the Phoenicians, for example—and sooner or later the know-how drifted back to Greece.

Like everyone else the ancient Greeks had pots for all sorts of purposes, from cooking and water-carrying to storing perfume or keeping the ashes of the dead. At a very early stage people began decorating their pots with geometric shapes[*] or representations of humans and animals, with special imagery for special pots, such as mourners on funerary urns. Initially (till about 530 B.C.) the decorating was done by incision and was mostly in black, with the occasional dab of red or white on the background clay color. Then the Athenians invented the technique of **red figure**, and also learned to paint. Now the figures could be drawn in outline, the background painted black and the base color left to show through. This allowed for more detail, so that the figures became more than mere silhouettes. The pictures grew more complicated, too, with scenes from mythology and also from daily life. A lot of what we know about life in those days is deduced from vase painting. Or, as Keats put it in his "Ode on a Grecian Urn":

> What men or gods are these? What maidens loth?
> What mad pursuit? What struggle to escape?
> What pipes and timbrels? What wild ecstasy?

---

[*] Including the swastika; it was perfectly respectable, once upon a time.

8

The Clever Stuff I: Math, Science and Inventions

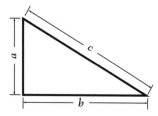

The things that the ancient Greeks invented, developed, classified and first thought of stagger the imagination, and they are basically the subject of this chapter and the next. We've already mentioned that Herodotus is considered the father of history; in this chapter we'll mention the father of mathematics (most say Archimedes, although he had two famous predecessors who might argue with that) and the father of medicine (Hippocrates). In the next chapter we can debate who deserves the title "father of philosophy," though one thing we can't deny is that it is an ancient Greek. And while we're at it, we'll look at some of the many ideas that the Romans took from the Greeks and improved upon.

So—no groans, please—let's start with the people who may have made you miserable in school: mathematicians and scientists.

Math and science

Pythagoras (sixth century B.C.): Most people remember Pythagoras because of his theorem (the square of the hypotenuse is equal to the sum of the square of the other two sides), even if they aren't sure what a theorem or a hypotenuse is. In fact, the theorem was probably developed by followers of Pythagoras, who was first and foremost a philosopher.

Euclid (fourth to third centuries B.C.): Credited with inventing geometry, for which I am sure we are all very grateful. In fact, his masterwork, *Elements*, organized the work of earlier mathematicians such as Eudoxus and Theaetetus and formalized the proofs of propositions that they had initiated. So if you spent part of your childhood proving that there were indeed 180 degrees in a triangle and writing "QED" (see page 19) at the end, Euclid is the man to blame.

Aristarchus of Samos (310–230 B.C.): Never heard of him? Neither had I. But would you believe that all those years ago he hypothesized "that the fixed stars and the sun remain unmoved, that Earth revolves about the sun on the circumference of a circle, the sun lying in the middle of the orbit," and that as a result the universe was vastly bigger than most scientists then thought? The quote is not from Aristarchus himself but from Archimedes (see next entry), who went on to trash the idea, with the result that Earth remained officially at the center of the universe for something like another 1,800 years. It would have saved a lot of trouble for Copernicus, Galileo *et al.* in the Middle Ages if Aristarchus's theories had caught on.

Aristarchus also made a brave attempt to calculate the distance from Earth of both the sun and the moon, and their respective sizes. I don't pretend to understand the calculations, but apparently his reasoning was sound; his instruments just weren't accurate enough to get it just right.

Archimedes (*ca.* 287–212 B.C.): Quite something. In addition to being the first man in recorded history to have really bright ideas in the bath, he was an expert in astronomy; he developed theorems for calculating the volume of geometrical shapes; he invented a water-lift known as Archimedes' Screw, which is still used to draw water from the Nile; and he may also have been the engineer behind the Romans' road-building scheme. At the end of his life, when no longer so friendly with the Romans, he was able to fortify the city of Syracuse in Sicily so powerfully that the mighty Roman army couldn't get in. He had concocted catapults that fired stones; cranes that dropped timbers over the battlements; and a claw-like device that pulled ships out of the water. Yet legend has it that he was killed during this very siege, by a Roman soldier whose challenge he ignored because he was engrossed in a mathematical problem.

Going back to the part about the bath, Archimedes is said to have been sitting there when he noticed that the level of the water was higher than it had been before he got in—that is, his body had displaced a volume of water, and therefore the volume of his body could be calculated. He may or may not then have leapt out and run naked through the streets crying "Eureka!" ("I have found it!") What he undeniably did was calculations about the water he had displaced. This turned into Archimedes' Principle: "An object immersed, whether wholly or partly, in a fluid is buoyed up by a force equal to the weight of the fluid displaced by the object." Or, if you prefer, W = pVg (weight = density x volume x gravity). It's important. Take my word for it.

Ptolemy (*ca.* A.D. 85–*ca.* A.D. 165): A Greek-born Roman subject working in Alexandria. The first thing to say about him is that he wasn't a pharaoh, although lots of pharaohs also were named Ptolemy. This one was, however, a great astronomer and mapmaker, and he did a lot of work on the supposed movement of the sun, moon and planets around Earth, so he must share the blame with Archimedes for consigning Aristarchus to near oblivion. Ptolemy also identified (or at least systematically recorded) most of the constellations we still recognize in the skies and produced an atlas of the world, which introduced the concepts of latitude and longitude to a wider audience. And if we had known that he also invented trigonometry, he would have been someone else we hated in school.

About numbers

Greek numerals seem to have been so complicated that it's a miracle the people using them managed to count at all, never mind invent all that math.

For a start there were two systems, the **Acrophonic** or **Attic** and the **Alphabetic** or **Ionic**. The Acrophonic took the initial letter for the name of a number and used that to represent the number. In other words, the word for 10 was *deka*, which began with a delta (Δ), so Δ was used to mean 10. This system had symbols for 1, 5, 10, 50, 100, 500, 1,000, 5,000 and 10,000, and mixed them together to make other numbers.

In the Ionic system, all twenty-four letters of the alphabet plus three more were allocated values ($a = 1$, $b = 2$ etc. up to 9, then $i = 10$, $k = 20$ and so on[*] up to 90, then $r = 100$ and so on. Then variants on these symbols were used to mean 1,000, 2,000, up to 100,000. So again, you put a string of symbols together to make any number you wanted.

Roman numerals derived from the Acrophonic system and consisted of:

I = 1	C = 100
V = 5	D = 500
X = 10	M = 1,000
L = 50	

Roman numerals introduced the refinement that you didn't only add numbers together, you also could use subtraction. In other words, whereas the Greeks counted

I = 1	III = 3
II = 2	IIII = 4,

---

[*] There was no *j* in the Greek alphabet.

the Romans decided that IIII was getting a bit cumbersome and substituted IV (one-before-five) to mean 4. Similarly more complicated combinations made up larger numbers, such as XCIX (ten-before-a-hundred, then one-before-ten) to make 99. Limited though it was, this system prevailed throughout Europe until the twelfth or thirteenth century, when it was supplanted by the so-called Arabic system we use today.

Medicine

The **Hippocratic Oath** used to be taken by doctors when they graduated and were about to go out into the world of practical medicine, but as it required the speaker to swear by Apollo, Asclepius, Hygieia and Panacea, it has rather fallen into disuse. It does, however, contain the still-relevant promise that a doctor will always do his best for his patients and not seduce them. I'm not joking—it does. Be they women or men, free or slaves. Anyway, I mention this because the Hippocratic Oath was probably invented by a man called...

Hippocrates (*ca.* 460–*ca.* 377 B.C.): The "father of medicine." Apart from the oath, his claim to fame is that he collected together a body of works known as the Hippocratic Corpus, which contained more or less all the medical knowledge that anyone had up to that point. His practice was based on the belief that all matter was made up of four elements—fire, earth, air and water—each of which had its own characteristics, later associated with the four bodily fluids or "humors": blood, phlegm, yellow bile and black bile. These in turn became associated with dispositions known as sanguine, phlegmatic, choleric and melancholic, respectively. The idea was that the four humors had to be kept in balance, so an excess of any of them led to ill health. This system was codified in the second century A.D. by **Galen**, a Greek-born, Egyptian-educated physician living in Rome; it was kept alive by the Arabs after the fall of Rome and formed the basis of Western medical practice for another thousand years, pretty much until the medieval Italians started studying anatomy and William Harvey discovered the circulation of the blood in the 1620s.

Going back to the oath, **Asclepius**, the son of Apollo, was the Greek god of medicine. (Apollo is also regarded as a god of medicine, but he had a pretty broad portfolio; see page 32.) Asclepius's symbol was the snake (because snakes slough off their skins and are thus rejuvenated), which is why a snake winding round a staff is still widely used as a symbol of medicine.

The cult of Asclepius came into its own in around 300 B.C. If Greeks were feeling unwell, they'd go and spend the night at an **asclepieion**, a sort of healing center. While they were sleeping, Asclepius would come in and heal them with the help of his snakes* and his daughters, **Hygieia** and **Panacea**, who were responsible for cleanliness and healing. And yes, their names are indeed connected with the word hygiene and with the synonym for a cure-all.

---

* Some *asclepieia* had actual live snakes slithering around on the floor to get people in the healing mood.

So what about the Romans?

The Romans were not only exceptional engineers and organizers, they were also fantastic developers and improvers. They didn't invent glass, for example, but they took up the technique of glass-blowing where the Phoenicians left off and were probably the first to put glass in windows. They didn't invent the spear or the javelin, but they improved upon them by making the shank out of a softer metal than the point, so that it bent on impact and couldn't just be chucked back by the enemy. They didn't invent armor, but they developed an articulated form that was both lighter and more flexible than anything that had gone before. And they didn't invent roads, but they invented the road system, so that they could get anywhere they wanted throughout their empire and keep tabs on any restless natives. Roads were built by legionnaires—soldiers who went everywhere on foot—so it was in their interests to keep them straight and make the route from anywhere to anywhere else as short as it could be. Being able to achieve this meant that the Romans were also pretty clever surveyors.

The structure of the army was brilliant, too, with the possible exception of calling a unit of eighty men a **century**, which was surely somebody's idea of a joke. Six centuries made a **cohort** and ten cohorts made a **legion**, which therefore consisted of 4,800 men under normal circumstances.* It

---

* In fact the first cohort was often larger, consisting of five double-sized centuries, i.e., five lots of 160, and one normal century, which meant that a legion could equally well consist of 5,400 men. Which is just what you might expect from a system that puts eighty men into a century.

sounds formulaic, but in fact the subdivision into small units made it very flexible: Soldiers marched and went into battle in strict formation, but each century could be redeployed quickly if conditions changed.

But they did invent some things...

One of the great inventors of the Roman period was a man known as **Hero** (or Heron) of Alexandria. Although he probably spent his entire life in his hometown, the existence of the Roman Empire gave his inventions the chance to travel throughout the known world.

Hero invented some pretty cool stuff for a dude you've never heard of. Some were really important to the future of civilization, such as an "inexhaustible goblet" that regulated the level of wine in it, or a mechanical theater with its own fire, thunder and drunken dancing girls; others were kind of transient, including an early steam engine (yes, really; forget England's *Rocket* from 1829; Hero was way ahead of him) and the first "fire engine."* This consisted of a hand pump that forced water out through a nozzle that could be adjusted to point in the direction of the fire. Hero also developed—but

---

* In the first century B.C., Crassus (he of the First Triumvirate, see page 84) became the richest man in Rome by the simple expedient of employing a fire brigade that would rush to the scene of a fire, buy the property at a knock-down price and only then put the fire out. This was before Hero's time, though, so Crassus's fire brigade relied on buckets and ladders. A system that was only faintly more sophisticated developed in London after the Great Fire of 1666 and led eventually to the emergence of both insurance companies and an official fire department.

probably didn't invent—a water organ that boasted the world's first keyboard (so forget Steinway and Moog, too) and the first coin-operated vending machine. It gave out holy water rather than condoms or multicolored candy, but that's probably because condoms and multicolored candy hadn't been invented back then.*

Another useful thing to emerge from this period is the odometer or "milometer." It was first described by **Vitruvius**, who wrote a ten-volume work on architecture in the first century A.D., but he suggests that it dates back to an earlier generation. Vitruvius's odometer (from the Greek, meaning "measuring the way") had a gear that turned another gear and dropped a stone into a box every time you had traveled a mile.

Vitruvius also wrote interesting stuff about **acoustics**, advocating the arranging of bronze vessels in a particular way around the theater to improve the sound. And, on the subject of theaters, the Greeks had already invented the proscenium arch, separating the audience from the stage and used in theaters to this day; the "wings" that hid performers from the audience when they were offstage; and the orchestra, originally a circular area in which the chorus sang and danced, refined by the Romans to a semicircle.

---

* The first recorded use of condoms in Europe comes in the sixteenth century, when the Italian scientist Gabriello Fallopio wrote that they helped guard against syphilis. Natural food coloring was probably in use in around 1500 B.C., but for the artificial stuff designed to attract children we have to wait until the early nineteenth century, when anything bright green probably contained both copper and arsenic.

Back to basics

Just as they were organizers and improvers rather than inventors, so the Romans were practical rather than high falutin'. So they made some pretty good **sewers**. Sewers and halfway decent toilets had existed in Knossos, Crete (see page 51), in 2000 B.C., but the Romans made theirs well, and they made them to last. The Pont du Gard in southern France is surviving evidence that they gave a lot of thought to transporting water—eleven **aqueducts** supplied water to Rome in the time of Augustus—and the Cloaca Maxima (literally "greatest sewer") existed as early as 600 B.C.

Most of the water supply went to—and the sewers came from—the houses of the rich, public baths, and public lavatories, where communal toilets sat over a channel that was flushed out by a constant supply of running water. You can see excavated examples of all this in York, England, and Pompeii.

Then there were the **baths**: hot baths, cold baths, something-in-between baths. They were a focal point of Roman social intercourse—and not always just social, if you believe all you read. The important thing here is the **hypocaust**, from the Greek, meaning "burning below." It was a form of underfloor heating that, among other things, heated the water for the tepidarium and the caldarium (think *caldo*—"hot"—rather than *cold* here). The idea was that you created a shallow basement under the room you wanted to heat and connected this to a furnace that produced a flow of warm air. A more sophisticated version also pumped hot air through tiles in the walls. Luxury.

9

The Clever Stuff II: Philosophy and the Liberal Arts

The word *philosophy* means "love of wisdom," and as a concept—understanding the meaning of life, and of right and wrong, and of what we can know about knowledge*—it seems to have emerged in ancient Greece, principally Athens, in the sixth century B.C. Vaguely remembered names from this period include **Parmenides**, who was overzealous about the concept of being and not being; and **Heraclitus**, who came to the not-very-helpful conclusion that everything was in a state of flux: Even the ancient Greeks called him "the obscure one." The first celebrity philosopher, however, appeared about a hundred years later. He never wrote a book, but he did do a lot of talking and his influence on later philosophers was immense.

---

* *Knowledge* in this context doesn't mean knowing the way to the supermarket or knowing how to boil an egg or change the tire on a car. We are in the realm of life, the universe and everything here.

The father of philosophy I: Socrates

We know—because everybody who wrote about him mentioned it and because there is a pot-bellied statuette of him in the British Museum—that **Socrates** (*ca.* 469–399 B.C.) was short, fat and ugly, but for the next few pages we are going to be above worrying about that sort of thing.

Socrates specialized in dialogues in which he challenged whoever he was talking to to justify their position on a given subject and then gently tore them apart. He never put forward a firm point of view of his own, but instead asked question after question in order to show the lack of wisdom (*sophia*) of his interlocutor. To be any good at talking to Socrates, you had to have a really deep, coherent understanding of your point of view, and be able to justify it rationally. So this questioning shouldn't be seen as negative and destructive; underlying it was a search for truth.

The way it began was that somebody had asked the Oracle at Delphi (always a bad idea) whether there was anyone in Greece wiser than Socrates.

"'No," came the answer. (Less obscure than many Delphic pronouncements, but troublemaking nonetheless.)

Socrates was shocked, because he knew that he wasn't wise, so he set about looking for people who were wiser than he was. He asked an important priest to define piety.

"It means honoring the gods and doing their will," said the priest.

"But we have lots of gods," said Socrates, "and our myths say that they often quarrel among themselves. If two gods are quarrelling, which of them do I honor?"

There was, of course, no answer to that.

Proceeding down this perhaps rather tactless path, Socrates questioned some of the most influential men in Athens, and came to the conclusion that perhaps he was quite wise after all, because at least he knew he was a fool. Unsurprisingly, this approach made him some powerful enemies, and he was eventually indicted for "not recognizing the gods which this city recognizes and introducing other gods" and for corrupting the young. He was sentenced to death and executed by being forced to drink hemlock. But his memory lingers on.

The father of philosophy II: Plato

Socrates's most famous pupil was **Plato** (*ca.* 429–347 B.C.), who founded a school called the **Academy**, where for the first time students were able to come together and study philosophy as a subject. Plato's approach broadly followed that of Socrates's dialogues, forcing people to think for themselves rather than simply accepting Teacher's point of view.

Plato is never a participant in his own published dialogues, so he always appears as one step removed from any views that are being put forward. This doesn't mean that he didn't have any ideas of his own, but they didn't really become famous until his philosophical descendants starting writing about them after his death. Perhaps the most important thing that Plato did was lay out a system of philosophy, based on rational argument.

Plato's own teaching (as opposed to that perpetuated by later followers) was in the Sceptic tradition. Different branches of **Scepticism** developed from this, the most important of them founded by **Pyrrho of Elis** (*ca.* 360–270 B.C.), who had traveled in India and may have been influenced by Buddhism. His stance was to refute as dogmatic any branch of philosophy that claimed to have found answers, because philosophical questions are so complex that suspending judgment and living by appearances is the only rational way. The cynical, taking-it-to-its-logical-conclusion approach to this point of view is that that big yellow buslike thing coming down the road may not be a bus at all, so you can cross the road anytime you like; the "living by appearances" part means that if it looks as if there is a bus coming, it's probably better not to walk under it. Even if it's an illusion.

Back to the man himself. His best-known and most controversial work is *The Republic*, which describes, among other things, his vision of an ideal city-state run by Guardians, whose lives were entirely devoted to the common good—they had no family life and no possessions. The concept was adopted by the Victorians to encourage young men (or at least the sort of privileged young men who were reading Plato) to devote themselves to public life, but in the twentieth century *The Republic* fell from grace and was criticized as proposing a totalitarian state that had uncomfortable resemblances to Nazism or Cold War–era Communism.

To treat *The Republic* exclusively as a political tract, however, is to miss the point, because Plato was also concerned with the idea of what makes a virtuous citizen, and indeed a virtuous person. The concept of virtue is an important one here, and we'll come back to it once we have touched on a few more schools of thought.

The Master: Aristotle

Plato's most important "descendant" was **Aristotle** (384–322 B.C.), who was born in Macedon, came to Athens and joined the Academy, then returned to Macedon on Plato's death and became tutor to the young Alexander the Great (see page 68). Once Alexander became king, Aristotle came back to Athens and founded a "research community" called the **Lyceum**, from which a lot of his research and lecture notes have survived.* For a thousand years (until Plato's work was rediscovered during the Renaissance), he dominated western philosophy: For example, in *Inferno* (written around 1307), the poet Dante meets a number of philosophers, including one "who is called Master of those who know." This Master is surrounded by, and being admired by, Plato and Socrates and all sorts of other people whom Dante names, but there is no need to name the Master—in those days it could only have been Aristotle.

---

* Aristotle's followers were also known as the Peripatetics, from his habit of walking around and around the garden while lecturing.

Aristotle's philosophical approach was to solve problems: to take questions that puzzled mankind and find ever more complex answers to them. He was interested in everything from metaphysics to biology, invented formal logic (see page 157), and viewed the adaptations of plants and animals to their way of life as an argument against a random creation of the universe. One book I read about him says that Aristotle's life was "ruled by an overwhelming desire to know." In short, he was a man who simply wouldn't have understood the words "Should I care?", even if you'd spoken them in ancient Greek.

He also had that rare commodity among philosophers: a smattering of common sense. Most of the others lived in and wrote about some sort of ideal world. Aristotle acknowledged that, although virtue was essential to happiness, it had to be considered in a concrete situation and as a mean point between two opposite evils. Courage, for example, should be seen as a sensible position somewhere between cowardice and foolhardiness. Virtue—and therefore happiness—comes from an individual practicing those qualities in a way relevant to his own circumstances. An oft-quoted example is that of the shoemaker who may be judged to have fulfilled his function in life if he makes the best shoes he can with the leather available to him.

Part of Aristotle's thinking is sometimes labeled **empiricism:** He believed that the active intellect (*nous*, a word the British still use to mean common sense or alertness) was somehow divine and, properly used, enabled us to understand universal truths. The empirical approach, however, made generalizations from the information available—through experience and the senses—and allowed you to get on with life while you struggled with universal truths. Plato didn't approve of this at all, but it worked for a lot of other people.

And just in case you want to quote him at a dinner party, here is my favorite Aristotle line: "Probable impossibilities are to be preferred to improbable possibilities." Perhaps best to wait until everyone is a bit drunk, though.

Other schools of thought

Also floating around in ancient Greece were:

- **Stoics**—so called because they met under a *stoa* or colonnaded porch—whose school (in both the physical and the intellectual senses) was founded by **Zeno of Citium** and taken over and developed by **Chrysippus**. The Stoics took a holistic approach to the universe, which they believed had been created by a rational god, and maintained that the wise man lived in harmony with nature (the stern commitment to duty that has given them a rather bad name came later).

- **Hedonists**, founded by a friend of Socrates named **Aristippus**, who believed in the pursuit of pleasure and the limitation of pain.

- **Epicureans**, founded by **Epicurus**, who developed his own form of hedonism by equating the concept of happiness with that of pleasure. This was at total variance with almost everyone else; we'll come back to these terms in a moment. He also differed from the others in rejecting the power of reason, which, he said, could lead you into error (in other words, even if you thought carefully about something, you could be wrong); only things experienced by the senses were reliable. That's empiricism again.

- **Sophists**, who weren't a philosophical entity as such, but traveled around "selling" intellectual skills such as rhetoric, grammar and ethics (which were certainly saleable, as they would be of great use to anyone intending to enter public life; more about them later in this chapter). Plato hated— and lampooned—the Sophists because he felt that by doing what they did for mere money, they were debasing the previously unsullied coinage of philosophy. The fact that Plato was rich and didn't at first take payment from his students may have had something to do with this. His view has stood the test of time, and we now define *sophistry* as "plausibly deceptive or fallacious reasoning."

That's probably enough schools of thought for now.

So what's all this about virtue, happiness and pleasure?

Well, lots of philosophers maintained that the purpose of life was **happiness**. They differed in how they defined the term. In fact, people still argue about the translation—the Greek word is *eudaimonia*, and there are those who think that "human flourishing" is a better way of rendering it. However, it's a bit of a mouthful, so let's stick to "happiness."

The important distinction is between the lasting quality of happiness and the transitory feeling of **pleasure**. Happiness meant a happy life, not a happy day or hour; and the road to it might involve sacrificing the (pleasurable) whim of the moment. The hedonist approach ran contrary to this: It advocated living in the moment—in other words enjoy the wine now, worry about the hangover tomorrow—which really wasn't a very philosophical approach to philosophy. Epicurus tried to get around this by defining two sorts of pleasure: the short-term kind we all understand (it tends to have booze/sex/chocolate in it) and the longer-term or "static" kind, which didn't get much more exciting than seeking tranquillity and a lack of pain. This may be why the word *epicurean* has come down to us as meaning "devoted to sensual pleasures, especially food and drink," because nobody was very interested in the more serious side of what he had to say.

The way to lasting happiness—at least according to Socrates—was through **virtue**. This was a powerful word that covered much more than sexual restraint. It meant an ingrained morality. Again, it's a distinction between the permanent and the temporary, between reason (always being a good person) and desire (only occasionally resisting temptation). And in the Socratic/Platonic tradition there is—crucially—a rational argument in favor of virtue: The virtuous person is a model citizen, and Plato's idealized *Republic* is an analogy for the internalized state in which a moral person can aspire to live.[*] In this ideal situation, the person's soul or psyche is under control and reason prevails over emotion.

A much-quoted example that may be of interest here is the story of Medea in Euripides's tragedy (see page 107). For revenge on her faithless husband, Jason, she murders their children—because, however horrific this may be for her, it is the worst possible punishment she can inflict on him.

In the play, she debates with herself: "I know that what I am about to do is bad, but anger is master of my plans." And indeed anger (emotion/desire) wins out over reason, and the children are duly murdered.

Now the Stoics, who saw the human soul as one united thing, would say that Medea had made a rational decision here—she acted premeditatedly, not out of blind passion. Plato, on the other hand, considered humans as tripartite beings in whom reason was always fighting to control desire and emotion (he uses the image of the charioteer—reason—struggling to control two horses, one of whom—emotion—will listen to reason while the other—desire—can be restrained only by force). So a Platonist would say that Medea's reason had lost the battle with her emotions, and she had acted irrationally.

You may say it doesn't matter much—the kids are still dead—but that is not an attitude that will get you very far with philosophy.

---

[*] This may be one of the ideas the antitotalitarians latched onto in the twentieth century.

Roman philosophers

There were other philosophers in the classical Greek period, but most of those who came after the ones mentioned above were followers of an existing doctrine rather than great innovators. The ideas were eventually picked up by the Romans, and it was common for a patrician Roman boy to have a Greek tutor, one of whose subjects would be philosophy. So the concept continued to be important.

Seneca the Younger (*ca.* 4 B.C.–A.D. 65): Son of, you'll be amazed to hear, Seneca the Elder, known as "the Rhetorician"; the Younger is known as "the Philosopher." He was a senator under Caligula but fell out with him (easily done), held a position at court under Claudius, was banished for allegedly having an affair with Claudius's niece Julia,* and then recalled to be tutor to Claudius's stepson Nero, over whom he briefly exercised a restraining influence once Nero became emperor (for more about all these emperors, see page 101 or just watch *I, Claudius*—it's available on DVD and worth every penny).

A life crowded with incident, you might say, but it didn't stop there. Nero, as every schoolchild knows, went more and more bonkers, and there was a plot to overthrow him. Seneca, accused of involvement, was ordered to commit suicide, which Tacitus tells us he did with extreme calmness, dictating a last few lines of philosophy to his secretaries after he had cut his own wrists. His parting words to his friends and family urged

---

* This is not the Julia with whom absolutely everyone had an affair; it's a couple of generations away, but they were still very active.

them not to mourn but to remember their maxims of philosophy.*

Marcus Aurelius (A.D. 121–180, emperor from 161): His philosophy survives in a book of *Meditations*, a collection of short pieces of self-scrutiny and "practical ethics." Marcus is full of advice to himself on how to be a virtuous person while performing his social role, that is, being a good emperor. He warns himself against "turning into a Caesar" and "being stained with the purple"; his aim is to be "good, sincere, dignified, free from affection." The Stoics were also hot on keeping emotions under control, and one of Marcus's observations on this theme refers to sexual intercourse, rather unsexily, as "the friction of a piece of gut and, following a sort of convulsion, the expulsion of some mucus."

It's ironic that Marcus, who worked so hard to be a Good Thing, should have produced a son who was so Bad that he (the son) was eventually assassinated. That was Commodus, played by Joaquin Phoenix in *Gladiator*,✝ the one who was so mean to that nice Russell Crowe.

A classical education

Yes, I know that's the title of the book, but it's also a useful way of introducing the three topics that, along with four

---

* Yes, really. Tacitus, *Annals* Book 15, if you don't believe me. Though to be fair, Tacitus was ten years old at the time of the incident, so possibly not an eyewitness.

✝ Marcus himself was played by Richard Harris, slumming it a bit before he was promoted to be headmaster of Hogwarts.

branches of mathematics, made up a liberal arts education in Greek and Roman times. These three topics—**logic** or dialectic, **rhetoric** and **grammar**—persisted into the Middle Ages and came to be called the **trivium** or "three ways," a word that was later devalued in English because these "trivial" subjects were regarded as the lowest common denominator of any school syllabus. It just shows how times change, because if you study philosophy at a university these days, you will come across logic and rhetoric.

Logic

I've mentioned elsewhere that there was almost nothing that didn't interest Aristotle. Whatever the subject, he liked systems and he liked classifying things, and one of the things he systematized was logic. He worked out a way of distinguishing between an argument that persuaded the hearer, and one that genuinely proved a point. Aristotelian logic relies on a **deductive inference** or **syllogism**, with the form:

All A's are B.

C is an A.

Therefore C is a B.

Aristotle was the first to use letters in this context to produce a general principle that could be applied to any proposition. The first two statements of the syllogism are called **premises**, the third is the **conclusion**.

For example:

> Blondes have more fun.
> Marilyn is blonde.
> Therefore, Marilyn has more fun.

Similarly, you can have the negative form:

> No man is an island.
> Peter is a man.
> Therefore, Peter is not an island.

If you want to convince someone that you know what you are talking about here, you can throw in the phrases **major**, **minor** and **middle terms**. The minor term is the subject of the conclusion, the major term is the predicate of the conclusion, and the middle term occurs in both premises but not in the conclusion. So, in my first example, "have more fun" is the major, "Marilyn" the minor and "blondes" is the middle term.

But your premises must be absolute; if they are not, the syllogism becomes what logicians call a **false deduction** or **fallacy**, that is, illogical:

> No man is an island.
> Helen is not a man.
> Therefore, Helen is an island.

This example doesn't work because, although you have stated that no man is an island, you haven't specified that everything that *isn't* a man *is* an island, so the move from premise two to the conclusion isn't logical.

The **undistributed middle term** is another example of a fallacy. In this instance, the second premise is not distributed in such a way as to make the conclusion logical:

> Dogs have four legs.
> My kitchen table has four legs.
> Therefore, my kitchen table is a dog.

In order to be logically correct—admittedly while demonstrating an alarming grasp of natural sciences—the last two lines of this syllogism would need to state that my kitchen table is a dog, ergo my kitchen table has four legs.

The best kind of fallacy, however, is called **post hoc propter hoc**. Yes, really. It translates as "after it, therefore because of it," meaning that if something has happened after you did something completely unrelated, you can take the credit. Praying for rain just before Wimbledon starts, for instance.

Most of this is laid out in Aristotle's treatise *Prior Analytics* (although he didn't use the Marilyn or Wimbledon examples). Then he came up with *Posterior Analytics*,* which is an analysis of the premises or "first principles" on which his syllogisms are based. There is a lot of complicated debate about the nature of knowledge (which blurs the already indistinct

---

* Sadly this title isn't remotely smutty in ancient Greek.

boundary between logic and philosophy), but what it boils down to is that the first principle or axiom must satisfy certain conditions if it is to be a basis for scientific knowledge. To quote the great man himself, "The premises of demonstrated knowledge must be true, primary, immediate, better known than and prior to the conclusion, which is further related to them as effect to cause."

For example, take the statement "Chocolate is good for you." Most women would treat this as an axiom: It is so universally known and glaringly, obviously true that it needs no further analysis. The occasional man, though, might say, "Well, that's because chocolate releases endorphins, which make you feel better." Pushing his luck, perhaps, he might then go on to say that "chocolate releases endorphins" is the axiom and "chocolate is good for you" an inference drawn from it. And actually a scientist would be able to demonstrate *how* chocolate releases endorphins, so that would become the axiom.

Oh, enough about that. St. Thomas Aquinas, one of the greatest of medieval scholars, wrote a treatise on the *Posterior Analytics*, and that's where you should go if you want to know more. He wrote it in Latin, but if you are the sort of person who wants to know more about the *Posterior Analytics*, I'm sure that won't put you off.

Rhetoric

The *Oxford English Reference Dictionary* defines *rhetoric* as "the art of effective or persuasive speaking or writing; language designed to persuade or impress, often with an implication of insincerity or exaggeration." It is really the first part of that definition that concerns us here.

Recognition of the importance of public speaking coincided with the emergence of democracy (see page 56), when being able to persuade a magistrate in a court of law or sway the crowd in a political debate suddenly had the power to make or break a man's career. (Before that, in the days of the tyrants, eloquence wasn't much of an issue; if the tyrant didn't like you, you'd had it, whether you had the gift of the gab or not.) So around the fourth or fifth century B.C., rhetoric became a subject of study, an accomplishment that could be taught and practiced in the same way as a language or a musical instrument.

It will come as no surprise—if you have been paying any sort of attention—to learn that Aristotle wrote a treatise on it. He considered three methods of persuasion: a) relying on logic, i.e., facts and inference; b) appealing to or playing on an audience's emotions; and c) convincing the audience that one is a trustworthy character and thus to be believed. Most rhetoricians would agree that logic is less important in oratory than the other two ways of swaying your audience.

This was precisely the skill that the Sophists peddled and that was so despised by Plato (see page 157): Rhetoric had nothing to do with a regard for the truth; indeed, you were a more skilled rhetorician if you could make the worse cause seem like the better one.

But if you really want to learn about rhetoric in the sense of swaying an audience's emotions, regardless of the facts, skip forward a couple of hundred years and read Cicero (see page 111). Cicero's speeches are wonderful and very readable examples of rhetoric and of the way in which Roman trials differed from ours—personal abuse of the accused (or the accuser, if Cicero was defending) and everyone and everything associated with him was a major and, to modern eyes, outrageous feature. Almost everything he said would have had Perry Mason on his feet yelling, "Objection, Your Honor!" Cicero was a great believer in oratorical training and technique; he rehearsed and rehearsed to perfect his delivery. As I said earlier, he was in many ways a man of great integrity. But once you got him into the courtroom, he really didn't give much thought about evidence—which is one way of defining rhetoric.

Grammar

Grammar as we know it was invented by Greeks from the Hellenistic period onward. Aristotle didn't write a treatise on it, for the simple reason that he was dead by then, but other people did, laying down the laws of syntax, parts of speech and the use of accents. Accents must have been pretty important in ancient Greek, because a man called Herodian wrote a treatise in twenty-one books about them, most of which, you'll be happy to know, are now lost. These Greek writers inspired the Latin grammarian Priscian, whose works, along with those of a later writer called Donatus, formed the basis of grammar teaching well into the Middle Ages. So all in all they have a lot to answer for.

10

A Bit of Light Relief: The Games

Gymnastic exercises, specifically running, jumping and wrestling, were an essential part of a Greek boy's education and—just to get it out of the way—yes, *gymnasium* does mean a place for exercising in the nude, and yes, that is what they did.

The Olympics

The original Olympics, which according to tradition date from 776 B.C. but are probably not as old as that, were part of a festival in honor of Zeus. They took place every four years at **Olympia**, on the Peloponnese—the place where the massive Statue of Zeus became a wonder of the world (see page 122), but not the same as Mount Olympus where the gods lived, which was way up in the northeast. As time went by, the games grew in importance and the program expanded from just sprinting to include long-distance running, the pentathlon, boxing, two- and four-horse chariot racing and more.[*]

---

[*] Mule-cart racing was featured briefly but was abolished as "possessing neither antiquity or dignity." Softball and baseball, which first entered the modern Olympics in the 1990s, have both been axed from the 2012 London program, though it isn't clear whether antiquity and dignity had anything to do with the International Olympic Committee's decision.

There were other pan-Hellenic games (meaning that people from all over Greece stopped fighting each other for a while so that they could compete), but none that rivaled the Olympics in importance. The Olympics themselves waxed and waned for financial reasons from about the first century B.C. and were finally banned in A.D. 393 by the Christian **Emperor Theodosius the Great**, whose greatness evidently didn't extend to allowing naked men to compete in athletic events.

By the time of the first modern Olympics, which took place in Athens in 1896, someone had found a way around the problem by encouraging the competitors to keep their clothes on.

Here's a little gem, courtesy of my beloved *Oxford Companion to Classical Literature:* Olympia is said to have been founded by **Hercules** (see page 39), and its stadium, like all the others in Greece, should have been 600 feet long (the word comes from *stade*, a measure of about 600 feet, which is a bit over 180 meters). This particular stadium was in fact a little longer because the great Hercules had paced out the 600 feet himself, and his feet were, naturally, larger than those of ordinary men. As Herodotus said (see page 61), "I am obliged to record the things I am told, but I am certainly not required to believe them."

And, just in case you were wondering, the Olympic torch isn't an ancient Greek invention: Every Greek city-state had a temple with a sacred flame that was never allowed to go out, and the Greeks held torch relay races, originally as a religious rite, and later as an athletics competition. But these weren't specifically to do with the Olympics.

In 1936, however, a man named **Carl Diem**, who was in charge of the forthcoming Berlin Olympics, came up with the bright idea of reviving the tradition. He proposed having a team of 3,422 young runners pass the flame from torch to torch along the 2,126-mile (3,422-km) route from the Temple of Hestia at Olympia to the Olympic stadium in Berlin. The lighting ceremony—with the flame lit by the rays of the sun—would be supervised by a High Priestess, as it had been in the good old days, and it would have acquired a vaguely sacred mystique by the time the flame reached Berlin. The PR man for these Olympics, by the way, was one Josef Goebbels—yes, him—and you can imagine that he loved the idea.

Roman games

"Now that no one buys our votes, the public has long since cast off its cares," wrote Juvenal in around A.D. 100. "The people that once bestowed commands, consulships, legions and all else, now meddles no more and longs eagerly for just two things—bread and games." The Latin *panem et circenses* ("bread and games")—an expression used to denote vote-winning freebies—is sometimes translated "bread and circuses," but *circenses* doesn't mean clowns and trapeze artists; it's something more like the World Series, or at least a high school track meet.

What Juvenal meant was that the people had lost interest in matters of state and had become fickle and irresponsible, and the only way to stop them from getting into mischief was to keep them well fed and amused, which is what the games were about.

The public (i.e., state-funded) Roman games were initially dedicated to a god, as the Greek games had been; later they were also held to celebrate an emperor's birthday or as part of the funeral of an important man. Private games—often on an obscenely lavish scale—might also be given by a political candidate looking to improve his standing with the electorate.

Unlike the Greek games, the Roman ones weren't full of naked athletes. In the early days, the main feature was a chariot race; later there were wild beasts and the gory stuff you see in the movies. The number of animals slaughtered was horrendous and only got worse under the empire; at a time when murdering emperors was commonplace, you couldn't expect many people to balk at the violent slaughter of a few lions and elephants.

The men who fought the animals were condemned criminals, prisoners of war, slaves or others hired for the occasion. **Gladiators** were drawn from the same apparently limitless pool of expendables, and their task was to fight each other. The name comes from *gladius*, meaning a sword, but only a few gladiators actually fought with swords. Most famously the **retiarius** carried a net (*rete*) in which he tried to tangle his opponent, and a dagger with which he could then finish him off.

Once a gladiator was floored by his opponent, he would appeal to the crowd for mercy, and this is where the much-maligned "thumbs down" comes from. In fact, turning the thumb down granted mercy; if the audience turned their thumbs up or inward, toward their chests, it meant "fight on," which was probably a bad sign for the guy who was already on the deck.

The **Colosseum** (see page 127) was the main venue for Roman games, but the **Circus Maximus**—which means "the biggest circus," or arena or stadium or whatever you want to call it— was the place for chariot races. The course was oval rather than circular, with a low wall down the middle and pillars at either end that the charioteer had to drive around. There might be as many as six chariots in a race, so there were plenty of opportunities for crashes and professional fouls. But you know that; you've seen *Ben-Hur*.

A final word

The 1959 film *Ben-Hur* won eleven Oscars, a feat that was unequaled until *Titanic* came along nearly forty years later. And why was the *Titanic* so named? Because she possessed titanic strength, an attribute of the Titans of Greek mythology, who existed even before the gods. As I said about 200 pages ago, the classics really are everywhere.

Cut.

Bibliography

Julia Annas, *Ancient Philosophy: a very short introduction*
(Oxford University Press, 2000)

————, *Plato: a very short introduction*
(Oxford University Press, 2003)

Marcus Aurelius, *Meditations*
(Wordsworth, 1997)

John Boardman, Jasper Griffin & Oswyn Murray,
The Oxford History of the Classical World
(Oxford University Press, 1986)

Thomas Bulfinch, *The Age of Fable*
(1855, Harper & Row Perennial Classics edition, 1966)

Paul Cartledge, *The Spartans*
(Channel Four Books, 2002)

David Crystal,
The Cambridge Biographical Encyclopedia, second edition
(Cambridge University Press, 1998)

David Ewing Duncan, *The Calendar*
(Fourth Estate, 1999)

Robin Lane Fox, *The Classical World*
(Penguin, 2006)

Robert Graves, *I, Claudius*
(Penguin, 1941)

Sir Paul Harvey, *The Oxford Companion to Classical Literature*
(Oxford University Press, 1940)

Jacquetta Hawkes, *Atlas of Ancient Archaeology*
(Rainbird, 1974; reprinted Michael O'Mara, 1994)

Herodotus, *Histories*, trans. George Rawlinson
(Quality Paperback Book Club, 1997)

Ted Hughes, *Tales from Ovid*
(Faber, 1997)

Peter James & Nick Thorpe, *Ancient Inventions*
(Michael O'Mara, 1995)

Alta Macadam, *Blue Guide: Central Italy*
(Somerset Books, 2008)

Nick McCarty, *Troy: the myth and reality behind the epic legend*
(Carlton, 2004)

Judy Pearsall & Bill Trumble,
The Oxford English Reference Dictionary, second edition
(Oxford University Press, 1996)

Nick Sekunda & John Warry, *Alexander the Great*
(Osprey, 2004)

Dava Sobel, *Longitude*
(Fourth Estate, 1996)

John A. Vella, *Aristotle: a guide for the perplexed*
(Continuum, 2008)

Virgil, *The Aeneid*, trans. W. F. Jackson Knight
(Penguin, 1956)

Philip Wilkinson, *What the Romans Did for Us*
(Boxtree, 2000)

All the classical texts I have referred to in this book (and many more besides) are available in translation on the Internet. Try http://www.fordham.edu/halsall/, www.tertullian.org or http://penelope.uchicago.edu/Thayer/E/Roman/Texts and just play around until you find what you are looking for. I also found a number of interesting things (by no means all of them relevant to what I was looking for) at itotd.com, where *itotd* stands for "interesting thing of the day." In addition, www.dl.ket.org/latin1/mores/law/citizenship.htm told me more than any of my reference books about Roman citizenship.

Dramatis Personae

Many of the people, historical or mythological, who appear in this book could have been included in more than one section—I chose, for example, to put Marcus Aurelius in the Philosophy chapter, despite the fact that he was also an emperor and could have gone under History. So this isn't intended as a comprehensive index (it's not that sort of book); it's just a list of the principal entries to the principal characters, because most of the ones most of us have heard of are in here somewhere.

Enjoy These Other *Blackboard Books*™

Featuring all the memory-jogging tips you'll ever need to know, this fun little book will help you recall hundreds of important facts using simple, easy-to-remember mnemonics from your school days.

$14.95 hardcover
ISBN 978–0–7621–0917–3

Make learning fun again with these light-hearted pages that are packed with important theories, phrases, and those long-forgotten "rules" you once learned in school.

$14.95 hardcover
ISBN 978–0–7621–0995–1

Fun and interesting facts and quips about authors and books sure to delight the bibliophile and make anyone the life of the literary party. Covering both modern and classic literature, this book will interest both bookworms and trivia buffs.

$14.95 hardcover
ISBN 978-1-60652-034-5

Confused about when to use "its" or "it's" or the correct spelling of "principal" or "principle"? Avoid language pitfalls and let this entertaining and practical guide improve both your speaking and writing skills.

$14.95 hardcover
ISBN 978–1–60652–026–0

Do you know who really designed and sewed the first flag? It wasn't Betsy Ross! The answer to this and hundreds of other fascinating myth-debunking facts of U.S. history will delight history buffs and trivia lovers alike.

$14.95 hardcover
ISBN 978–1–60652–035–2